NOCTURNES
AND POLONAISES

Frédéric Chopin

NOCTURNES AND POLONAISES

The Paderewski Edition

edited by
Ignacy Jan Paderewski
Ludwik Bronarski
Józef Turczyński

Dover Publications, Inc., New York

This Dover edition, first published in 1983, contains all the music and commentary from Volume VII, *Nocturnes for Piano* (1951), and Volume VIII, *Polonaises for Piano* (1951), of the work *Fryderyk Chopin/ Complete Works*, published by the Fryderyk Chopin Institute/Polish Music Publications (Institut Fryderyka Chopina/Polskie Wydawnictwo Muzyczne). The illustrations in the original volumes have been omitted, and a new unified table of contents has been substituted for the two original tables of incipits.

Manufactured in the United States of America
Dover Publications, Inc., 31 East 2nd Street, Mineola, N.Y. 11501

Library of Congress Cataloging in Publication Data

Chopin, Frédéric, 1810–1849.
  [Piano music. Selections]
  Nocturnes ; and, Polonaises.

  For piano.
  Reprint. Originally published: Warsaw : Fryderyk Chopin Institute, 1951. (Complete works / Fryderyk Chopin ; v. 7–8)
  1. Piano music. 2. Polonaises (Piano)
I. Paderewski, Ignace Jan, 1860–1941. II. Bronarski, Ludwik, 1890–
   . III. Turczyński, Józef. IV. Chopin, Frédéric, 1810–1849. Nocturnes, piano. 1983. V. Chopin, Frédéric, 1810–1849. Polonaises, piano. 1983.
M22.C545P22   1983   83-5276
ISBN 0-486-24564-0

CONTENTS

Nocturnes

Polonaises

Note: The following Nocturnes listed in the 1980 edition of *Grove* are not included here: C-sharp Minor (1830; published 1875), and C Minor (1837; published 1938).

NOCTURNES AND POLONAISES

A Madame Camille Pleyel

TROIS NOCTURNES

FR. CHOPIN
Op. 9   Nr 1

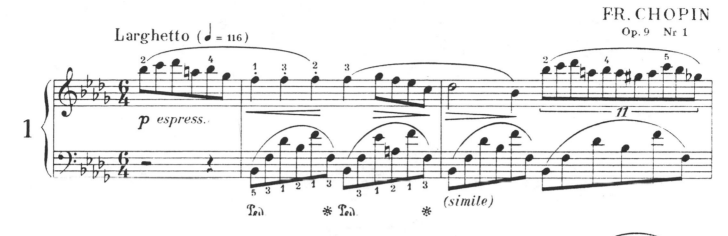

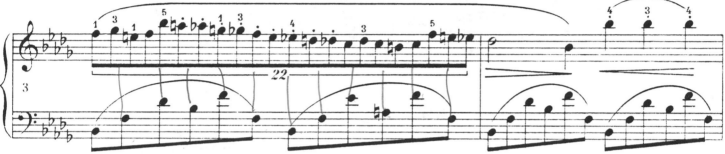

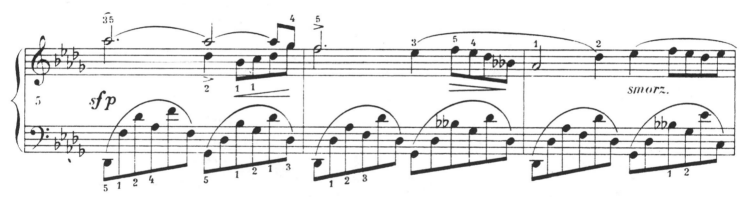

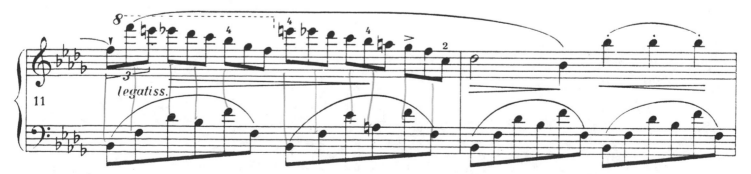

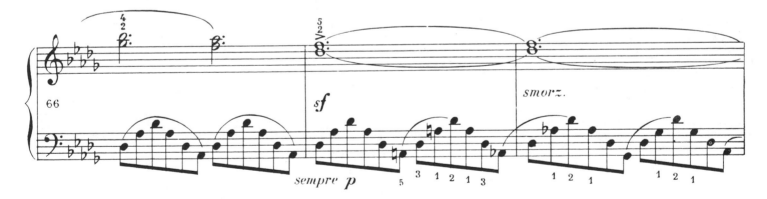

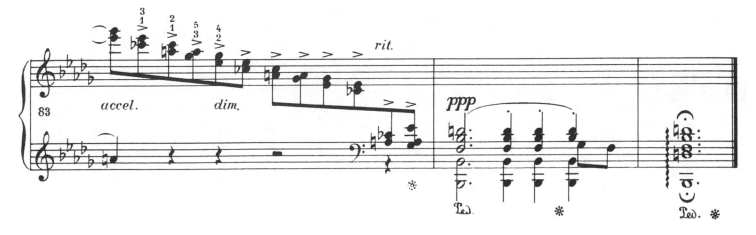

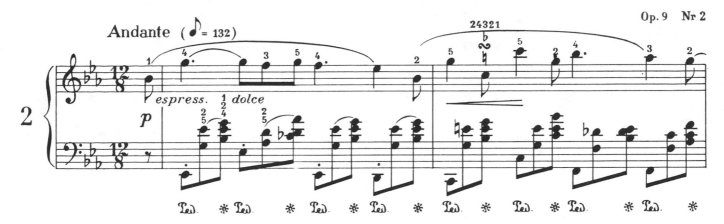

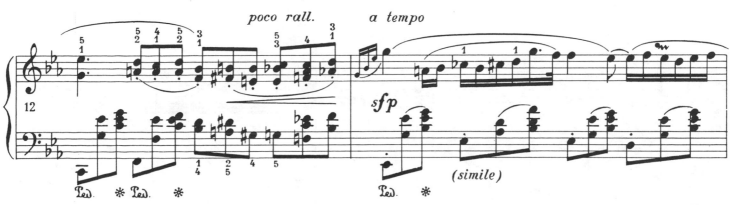

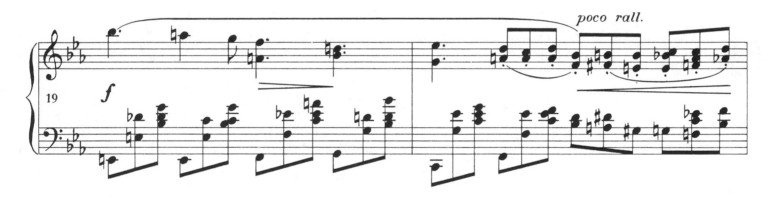

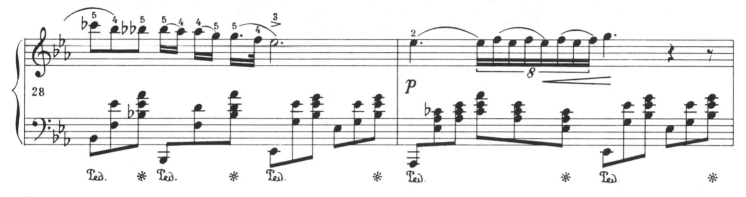

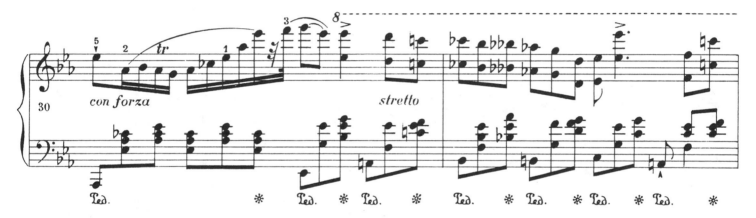

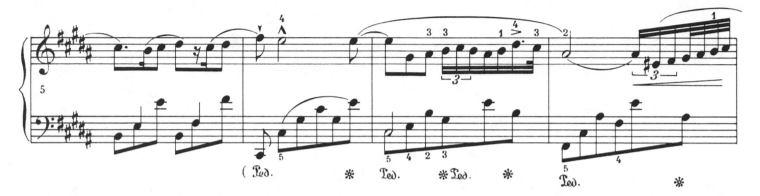

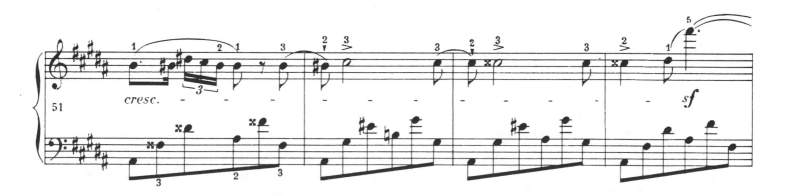

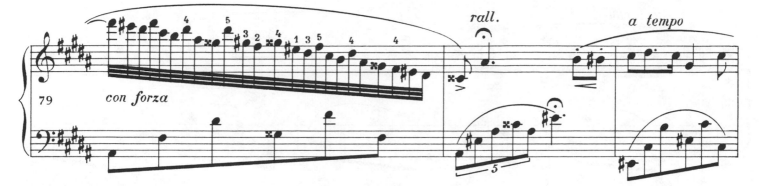

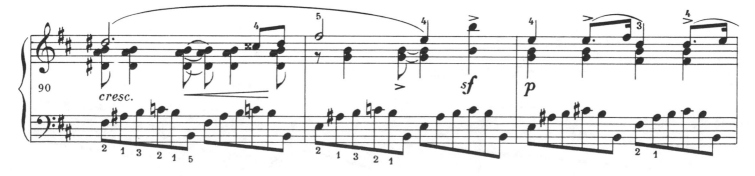

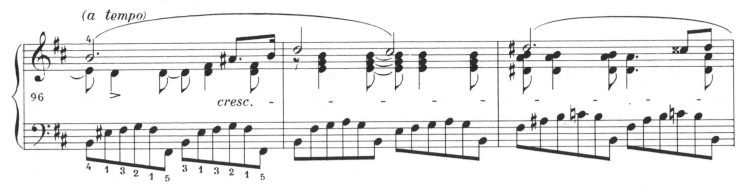

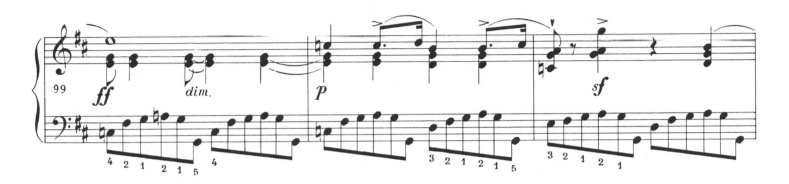

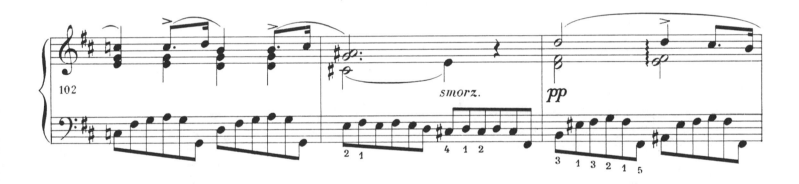

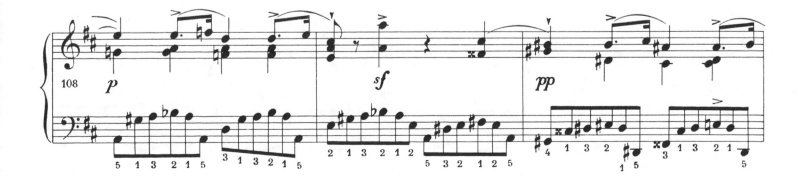

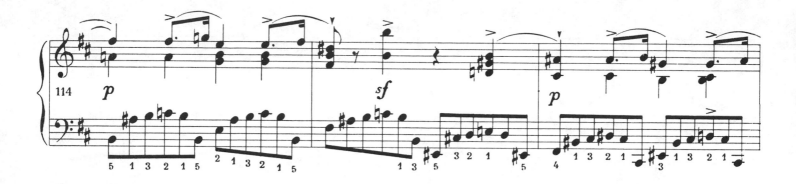

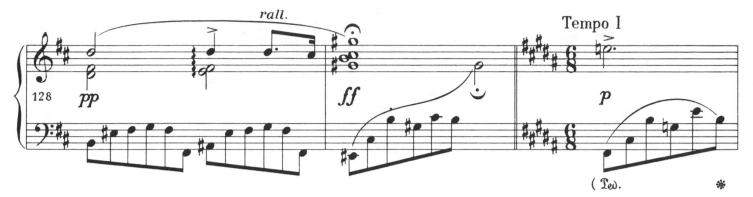

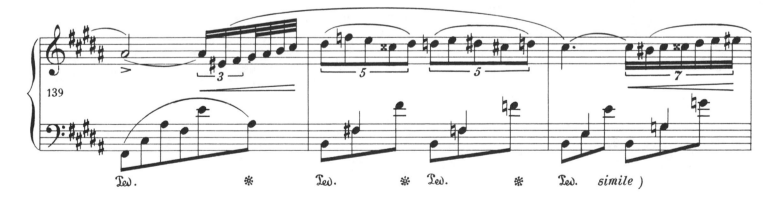

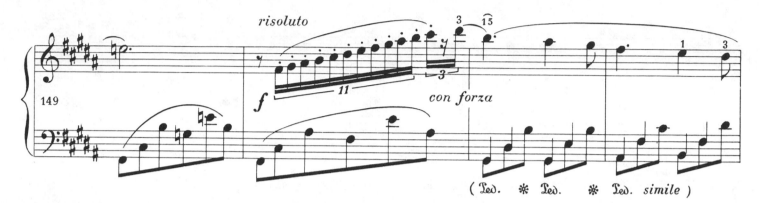

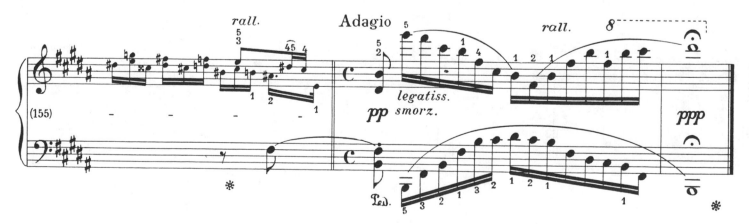

A Monsieur F. Hiller

TROIS NOCTURNES

Andante cantabile (♩ = 69)

Op. 15 Nr 1

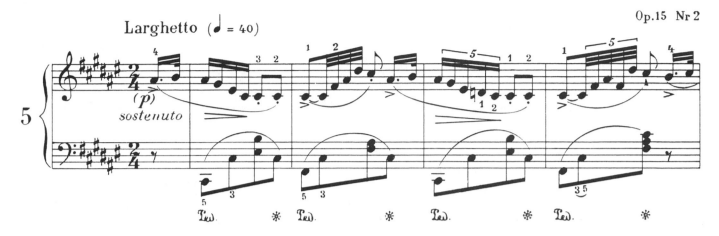

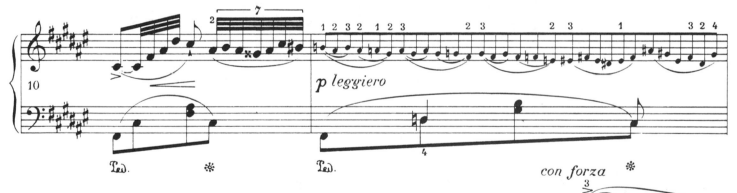

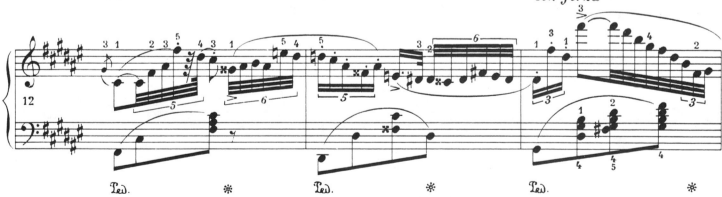

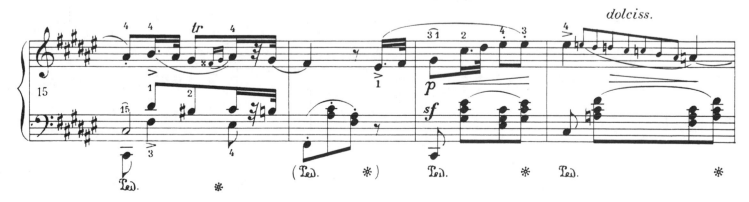

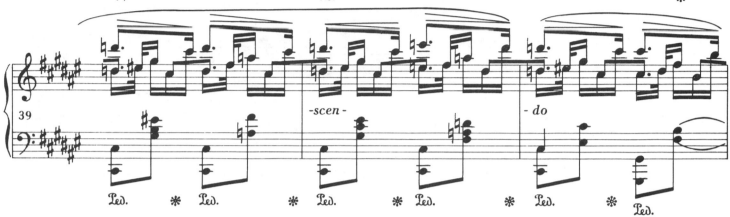

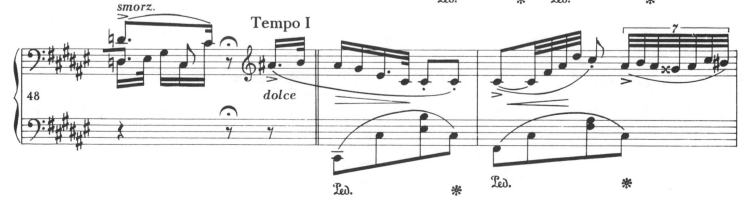

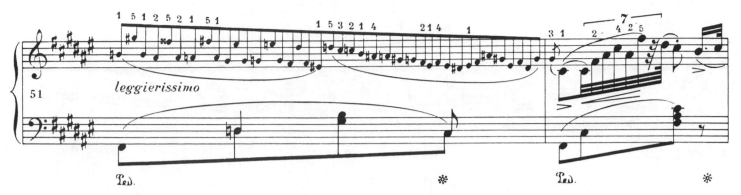

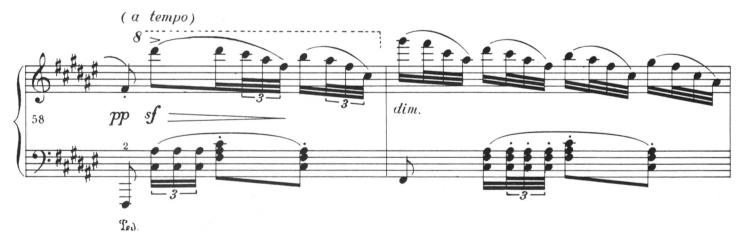

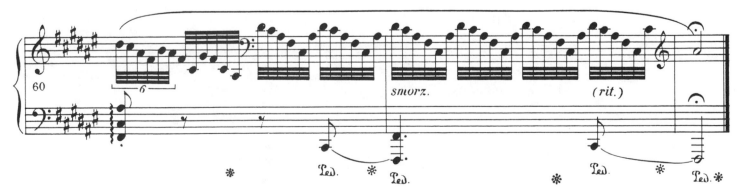

Op. 15 Nr 3

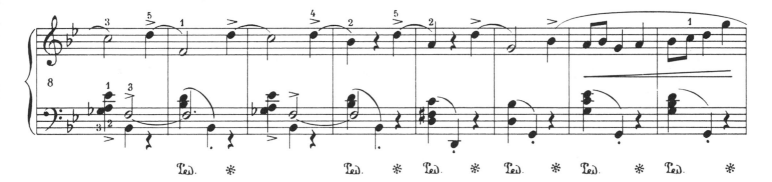

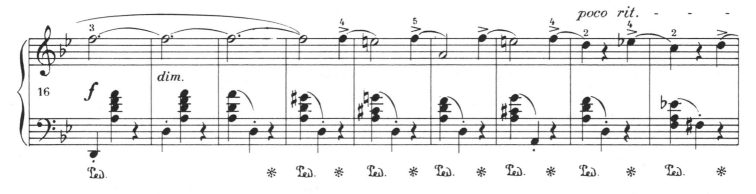

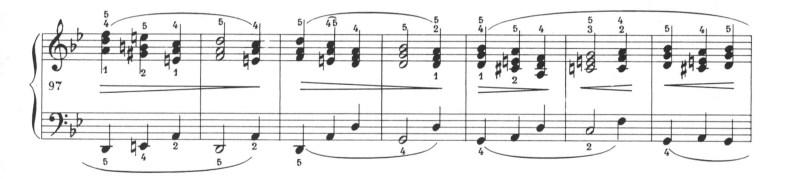

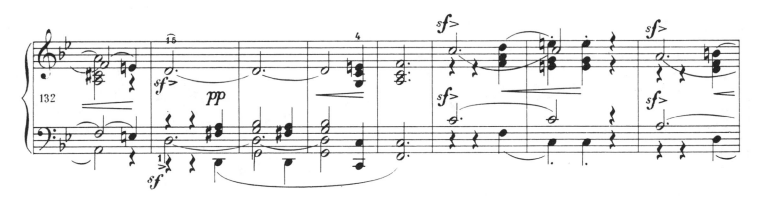

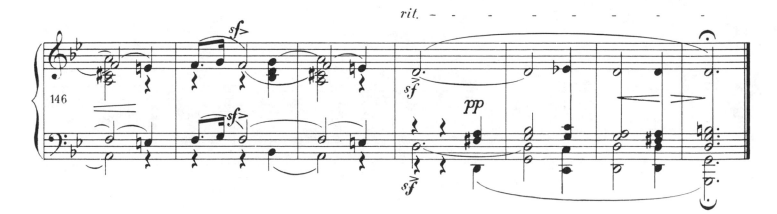

A Madame la Comtesse d'Appony

DEUX NOCTURNES

Op. 27 Nr 1

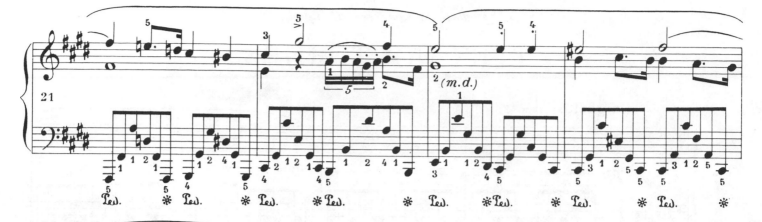

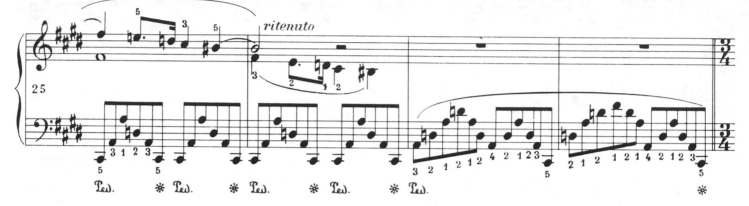

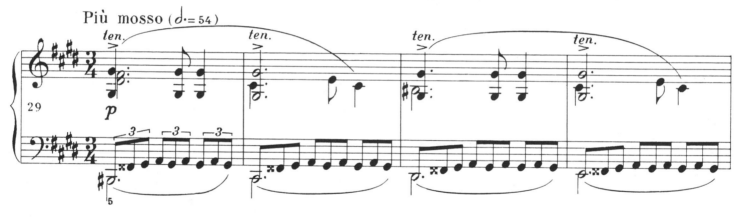

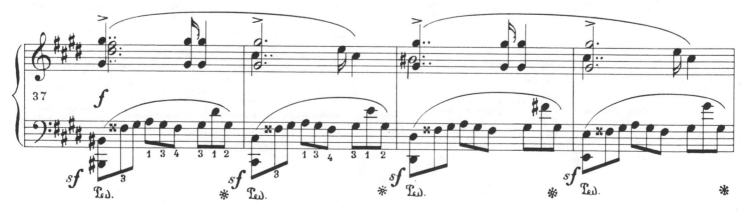

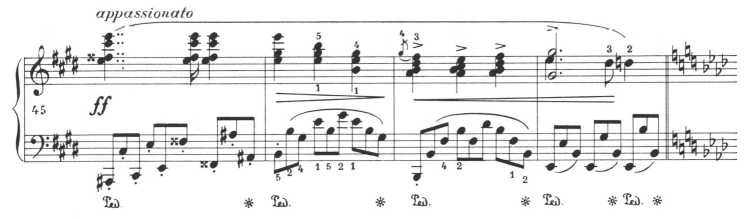

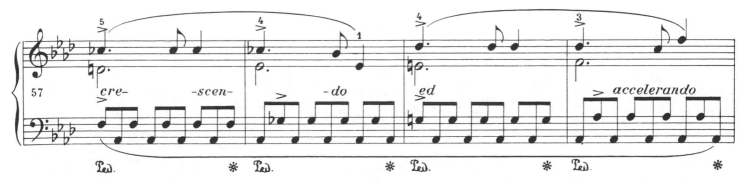

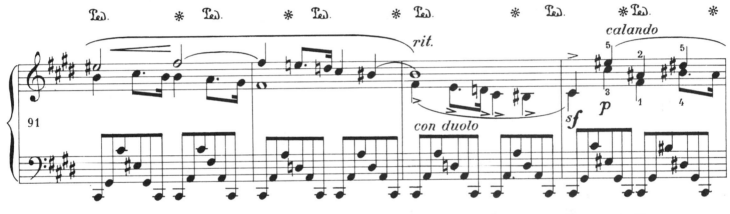

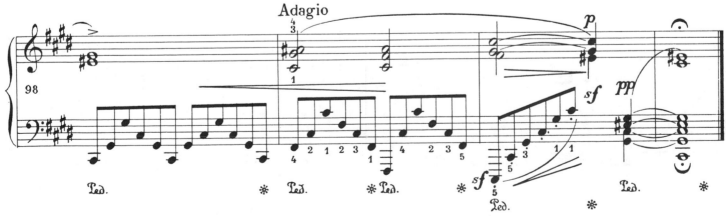

Op. 27 Nr 2

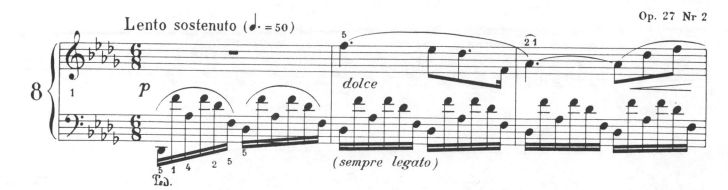

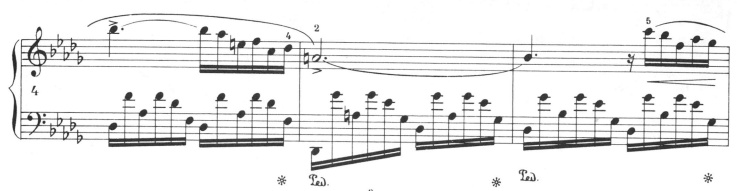

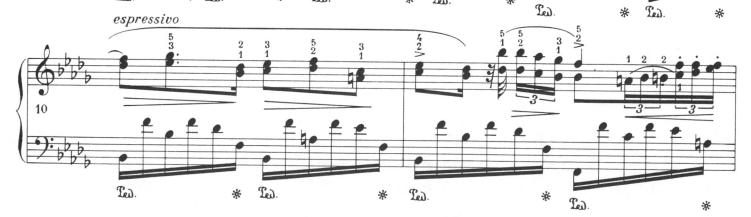

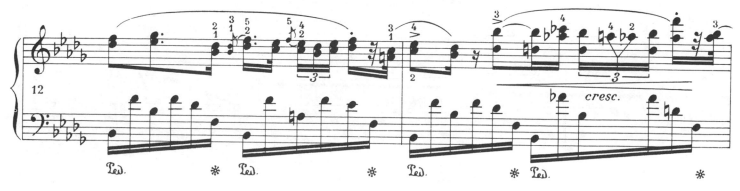

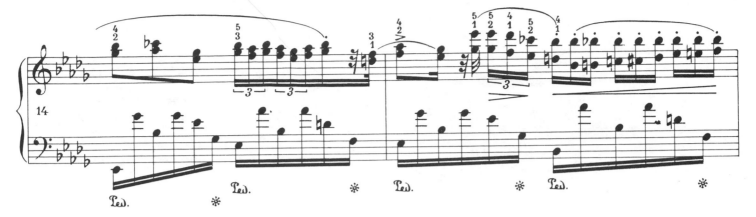

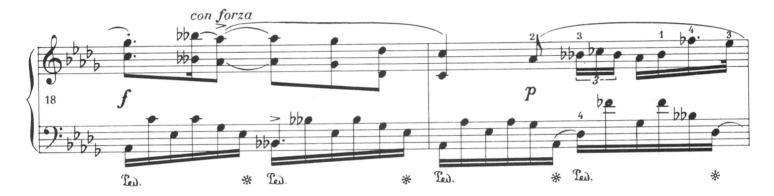

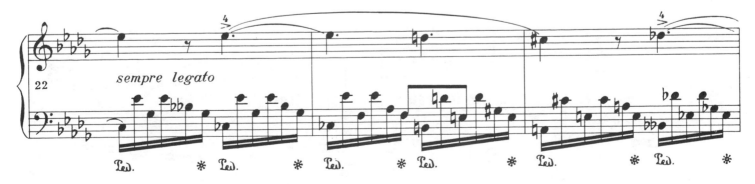

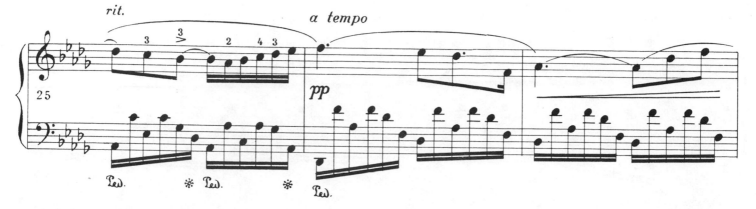

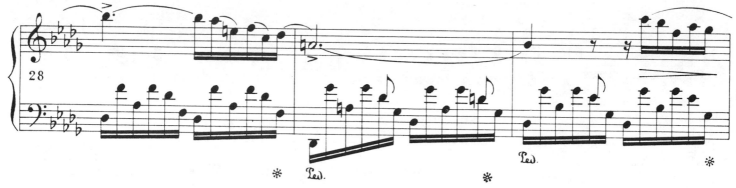

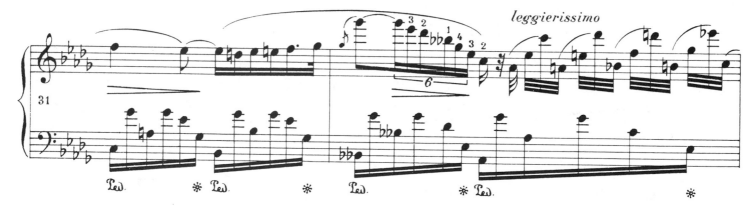

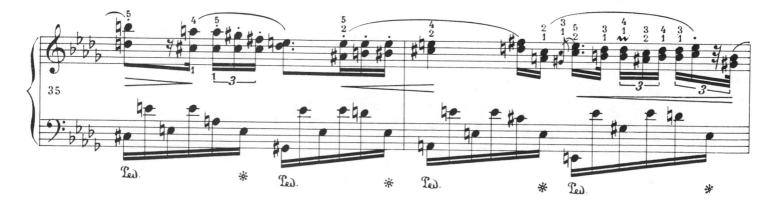

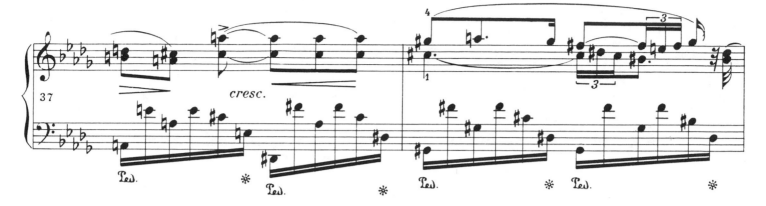

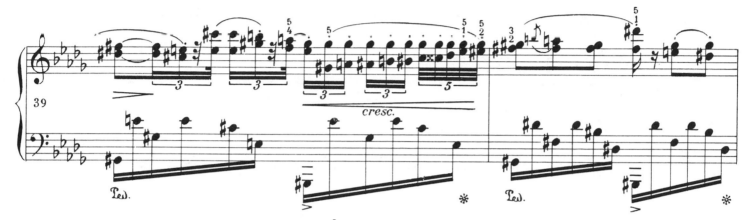

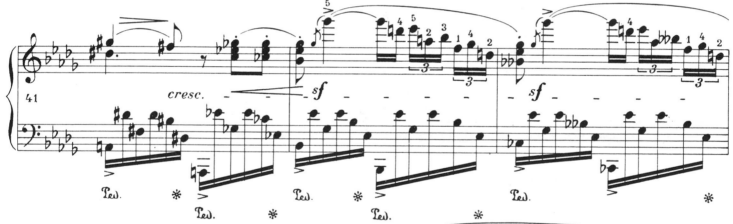

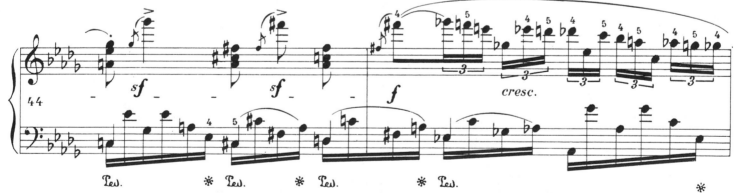

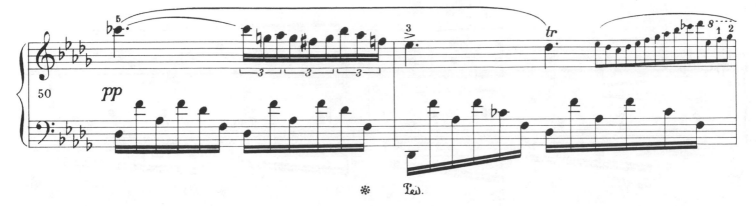

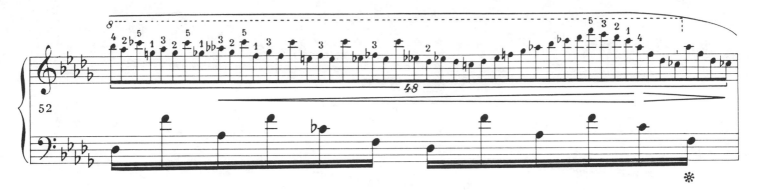

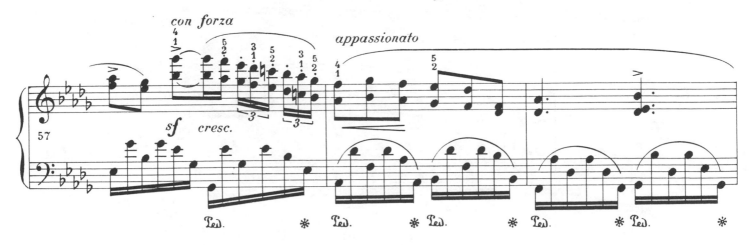

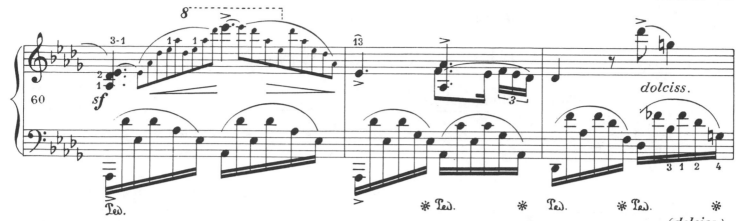

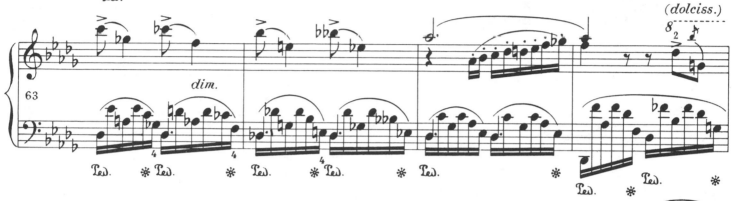

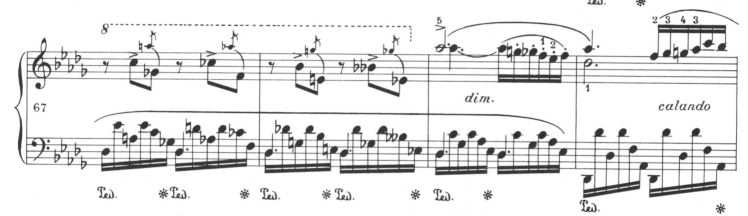

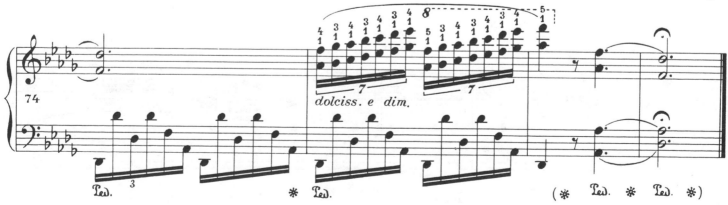

A Madame la Baronne de Billing, née de Courbonne

DEUX NOCTURNES

Op. 32　Nr 1

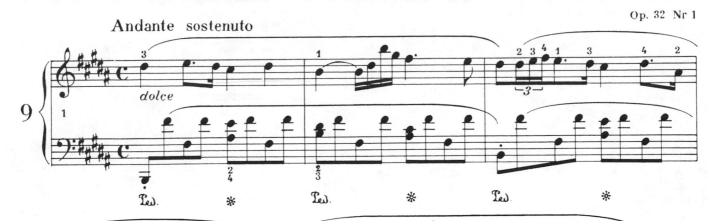

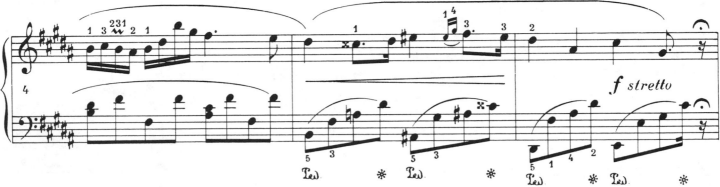

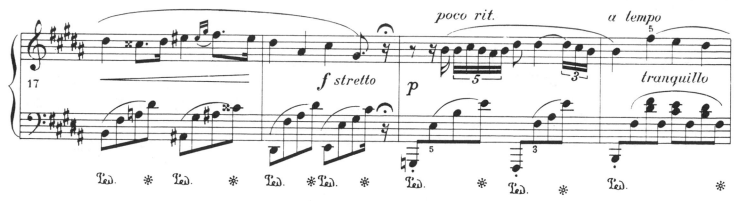

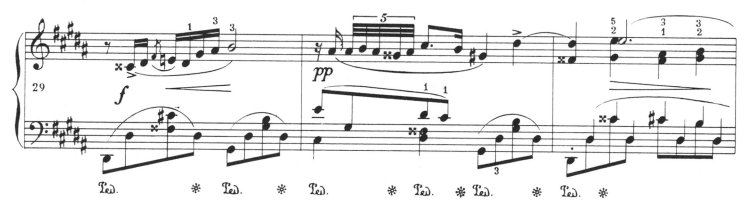

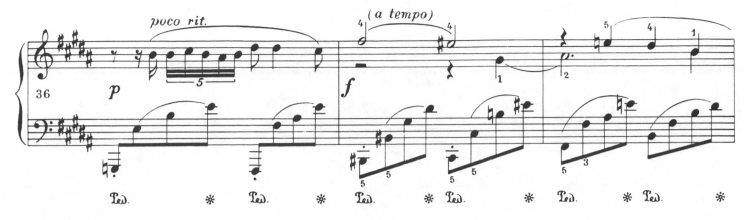

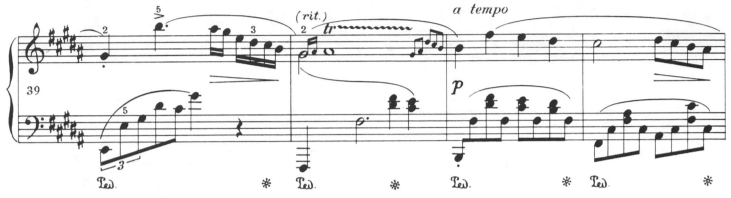

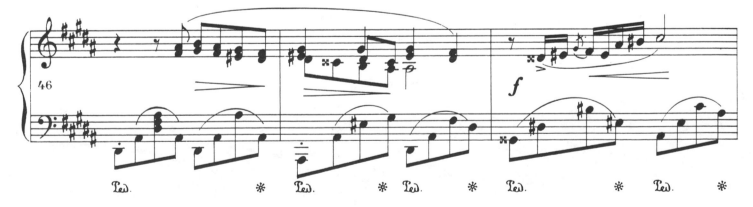

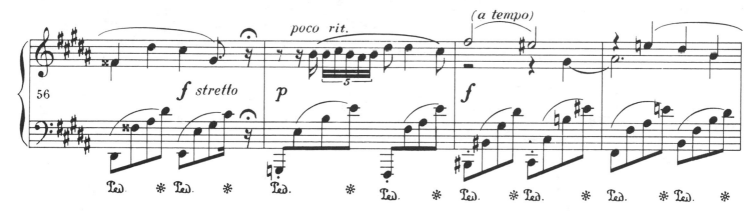

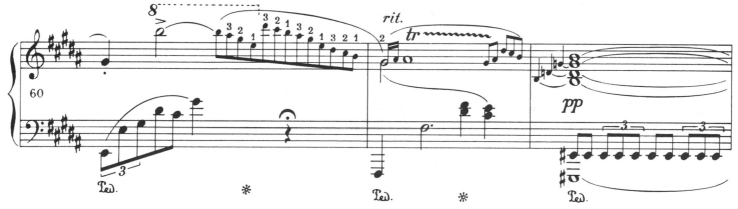

Op. 32 Nr 2

Lento

10

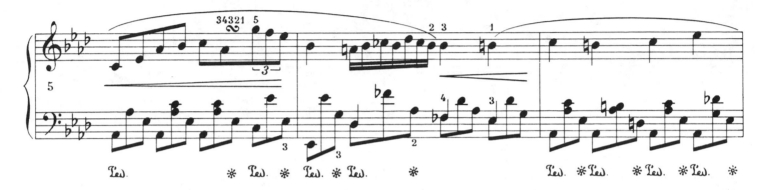

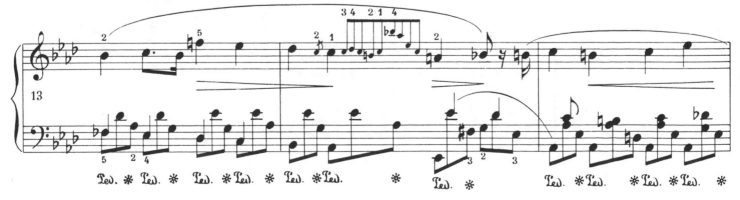

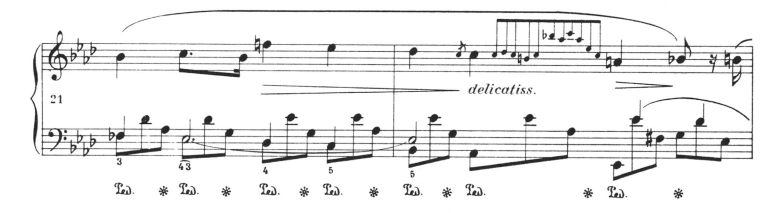

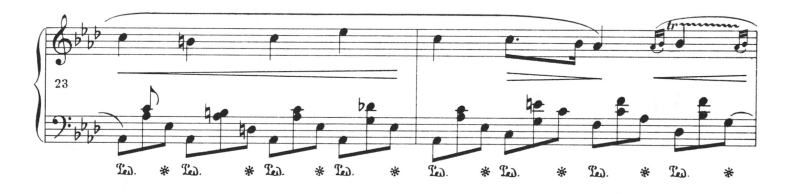

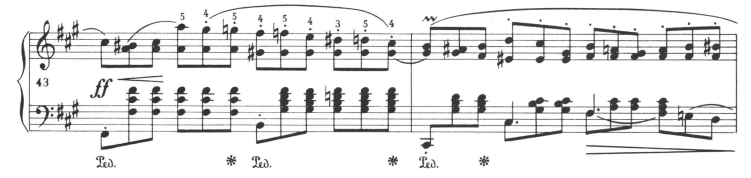

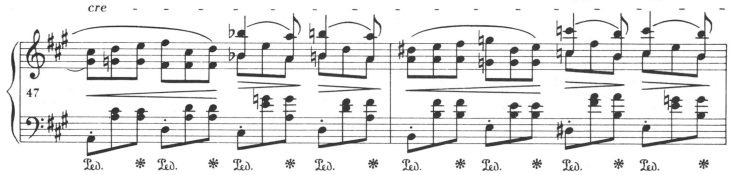

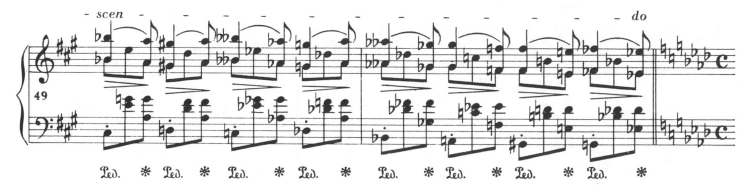

Appassionato

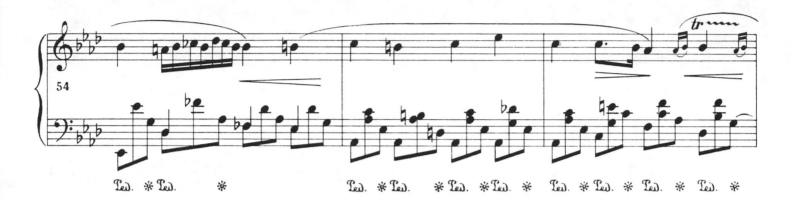

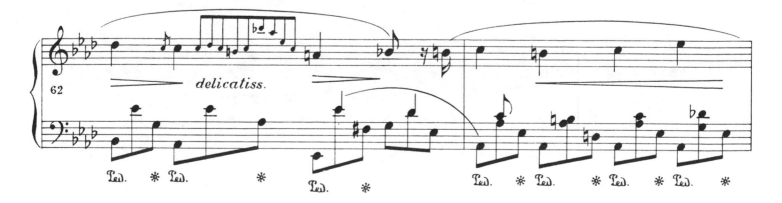

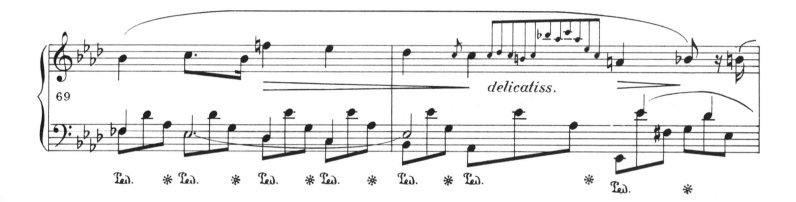

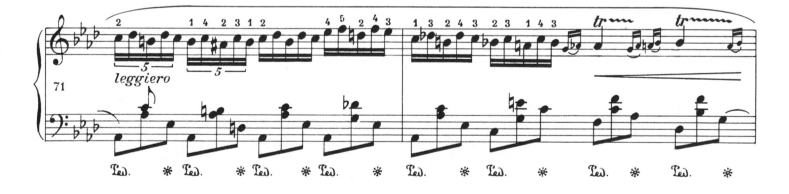

DEUX NOCTURNES

Op. 37 Nr 1

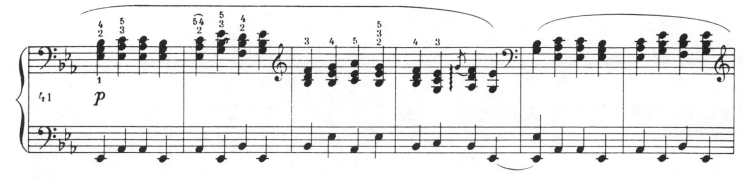

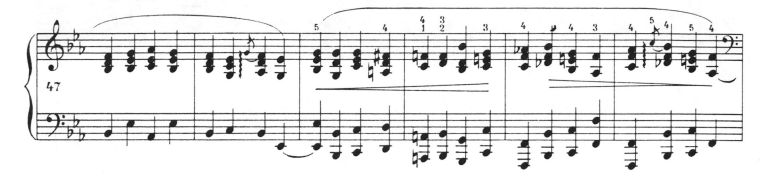

Op. 37 Nr 2

12

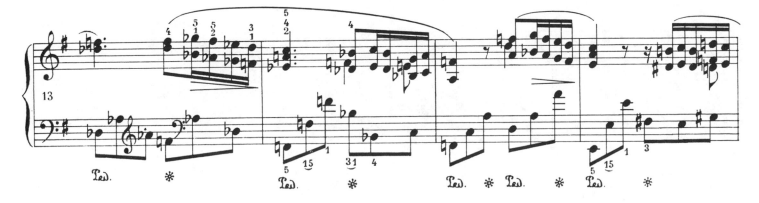

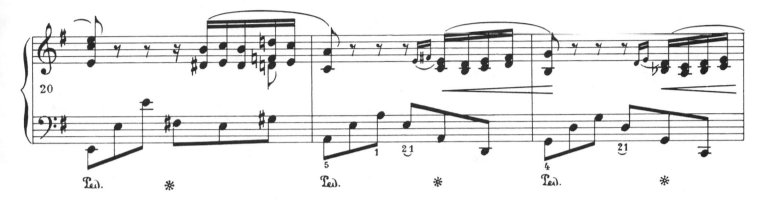

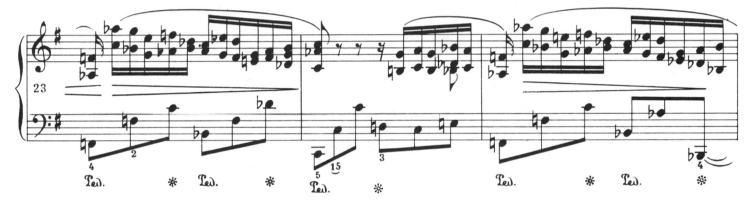

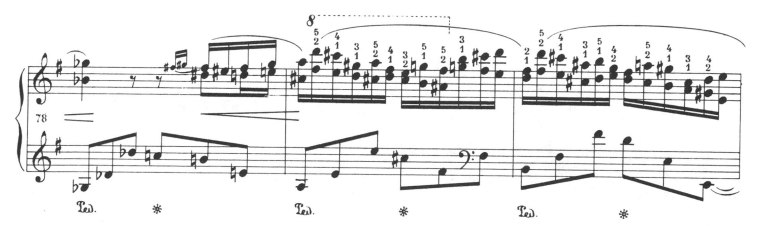

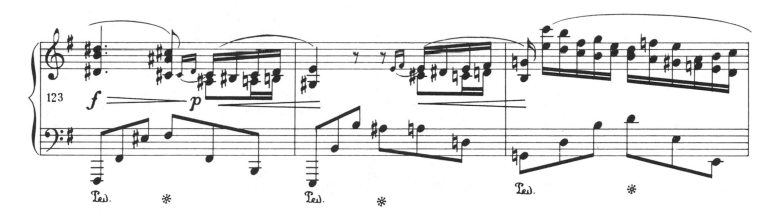

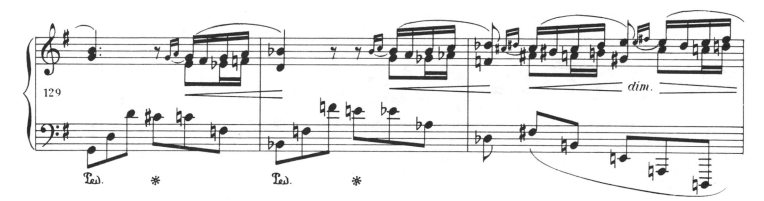

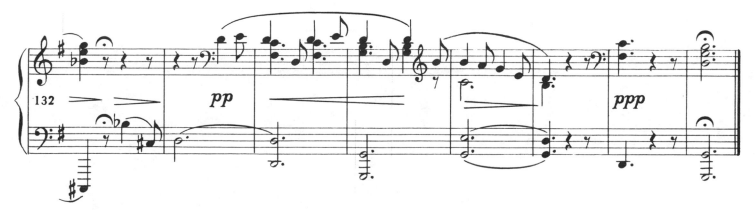

A Mademoiselle Laure Duperré

DEUX NOCTURNES

Op. 48 Nr 1

13

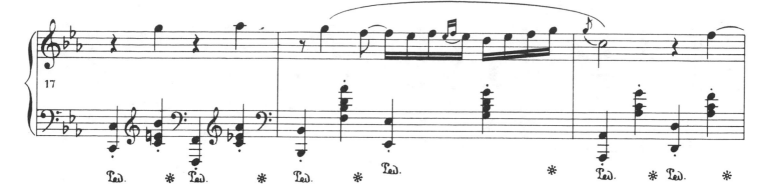

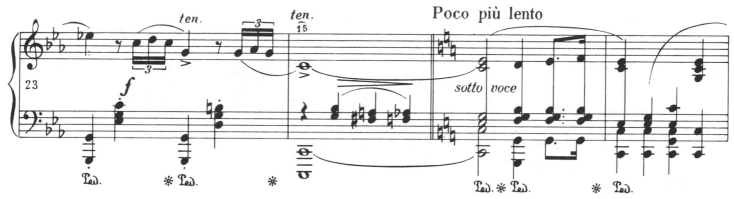

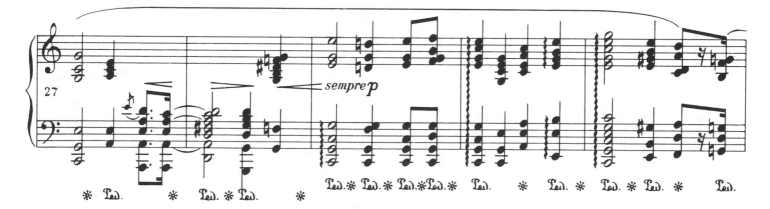

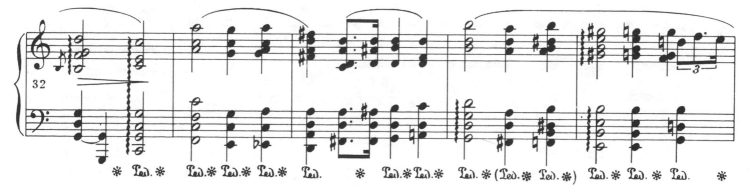

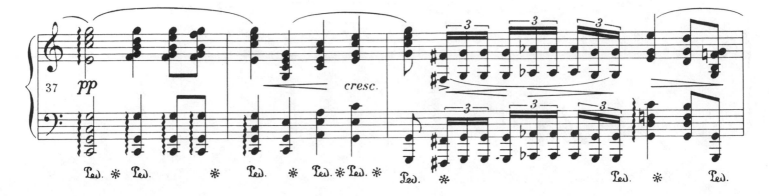

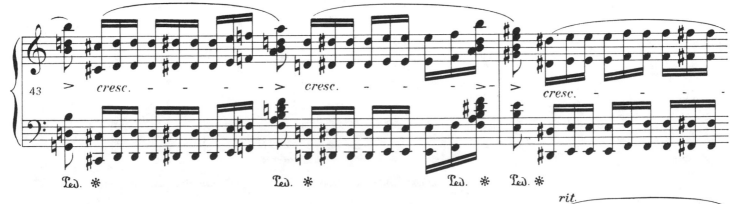

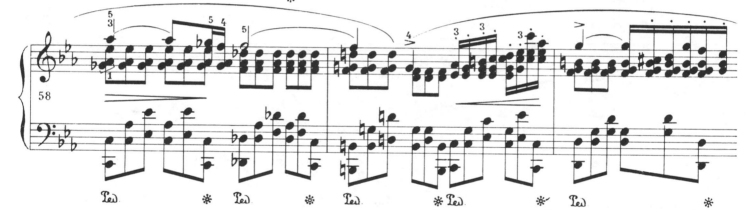

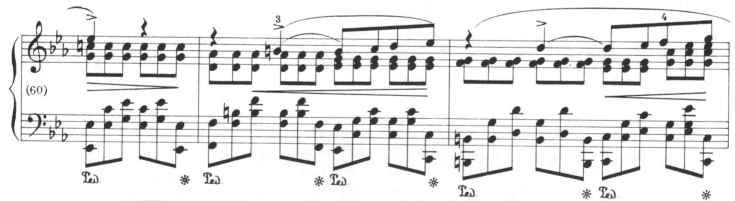

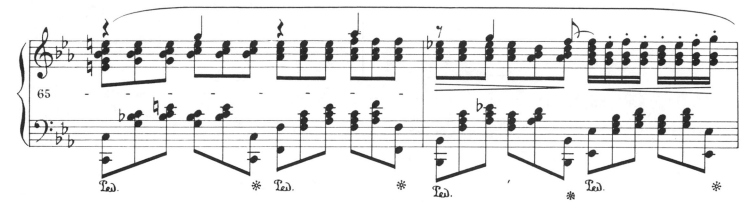

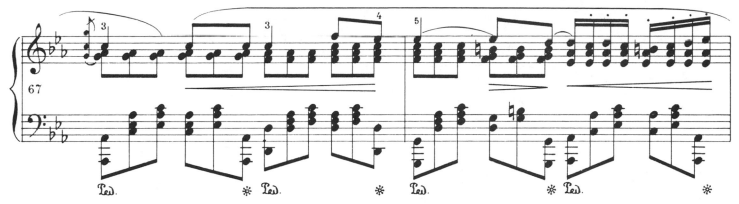

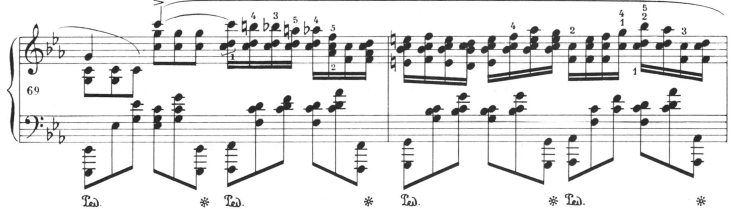

Op. 48 Nr 2

Andantino

14

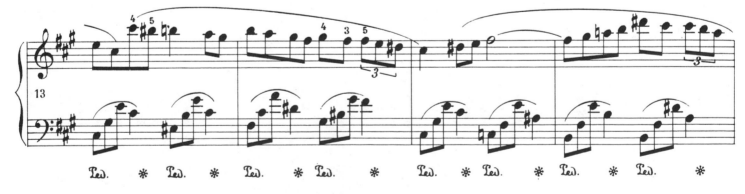

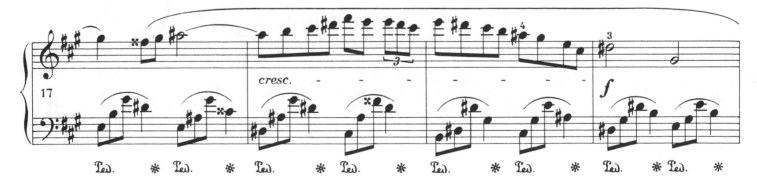

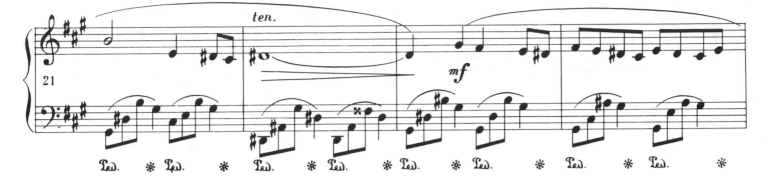

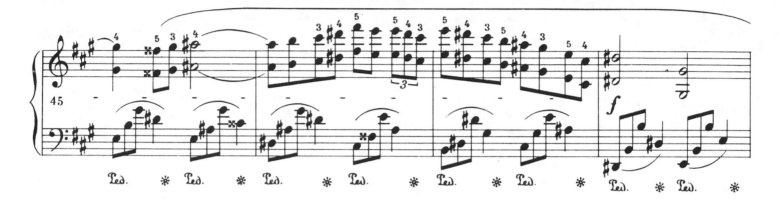

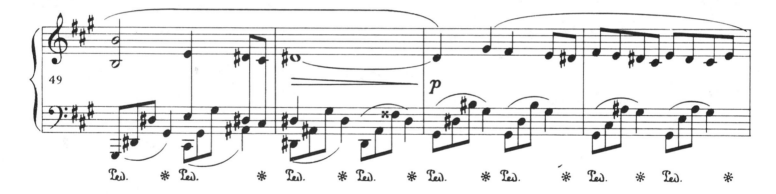

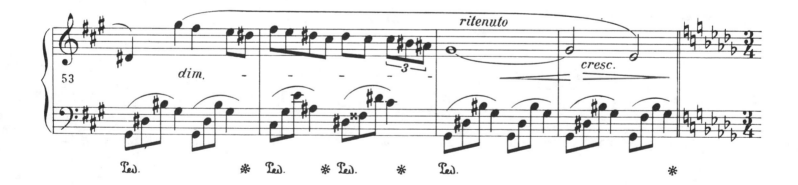

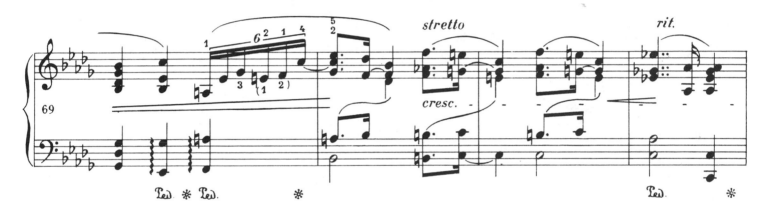

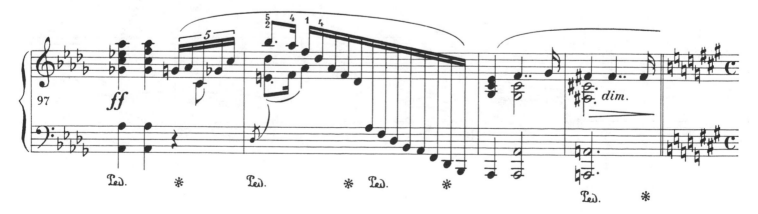

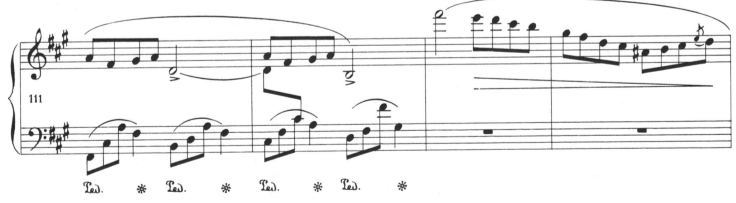

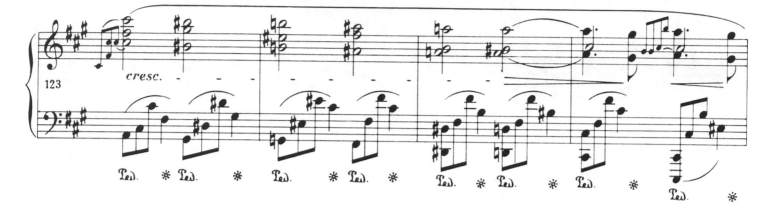

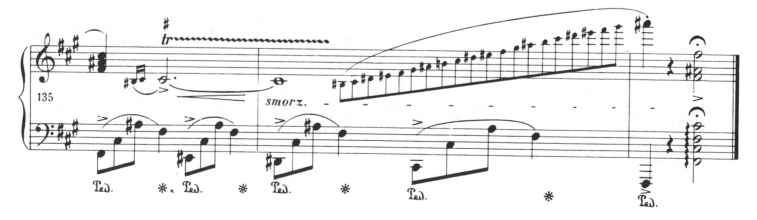

A Mademoiselle J.W. Stirling

DEUX NOCTURNES

Op. 55 Nr 1

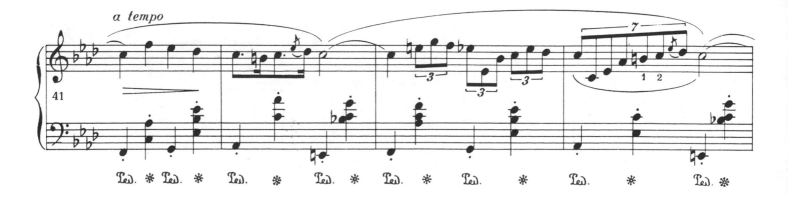

Più mosso

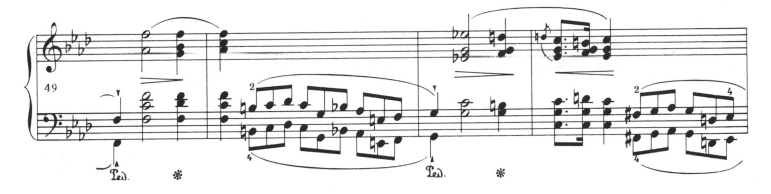

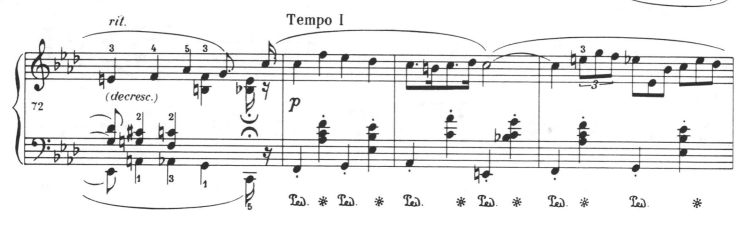

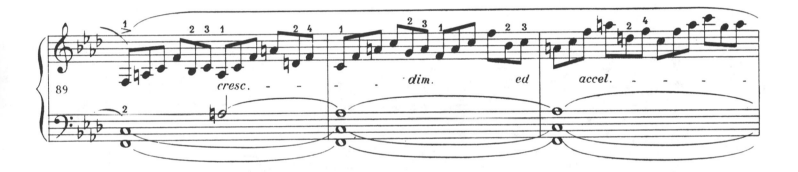

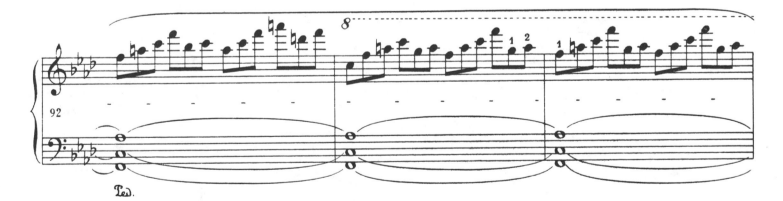

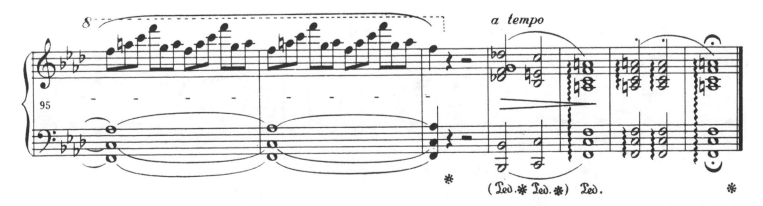

Lento sostenuto

Op. 55 Nr 2

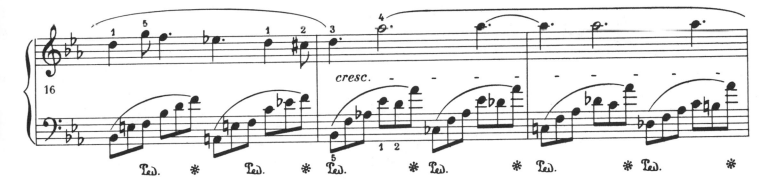

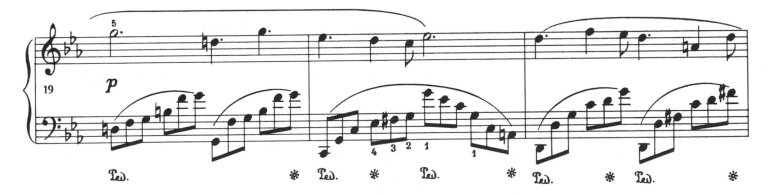

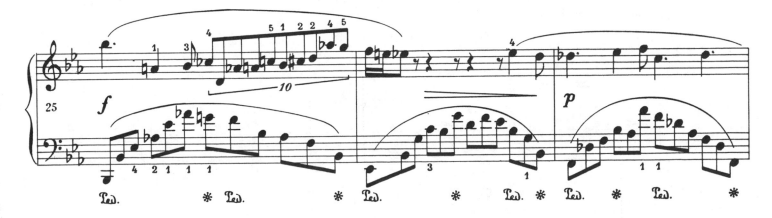

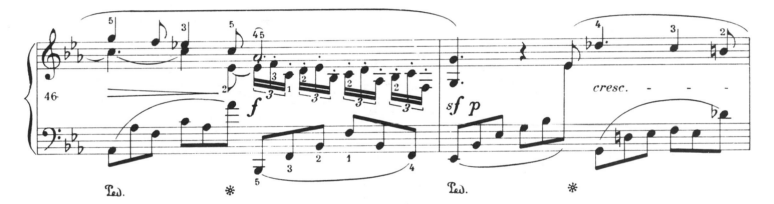

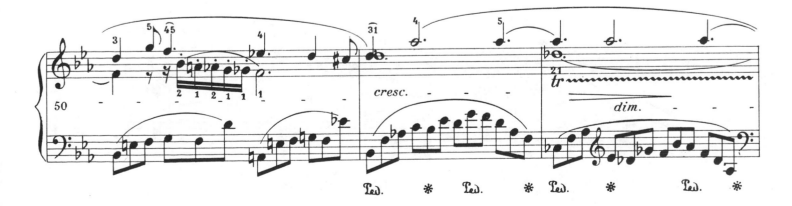

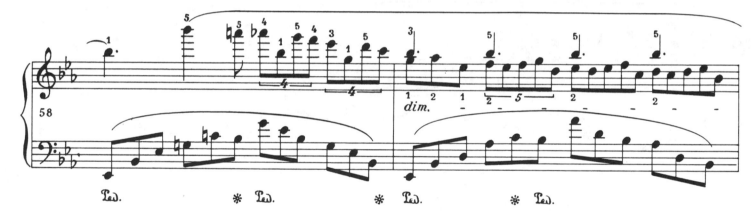

A Mademoiselle R. de Könneritz

DEUX NOCTURNES

Op. 62 Nr 1

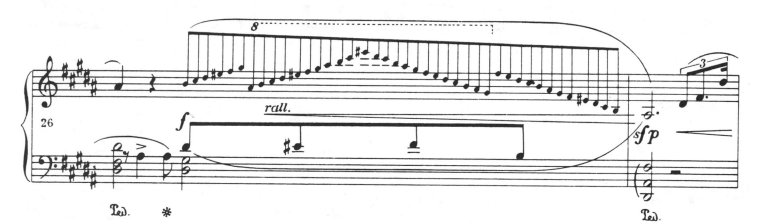

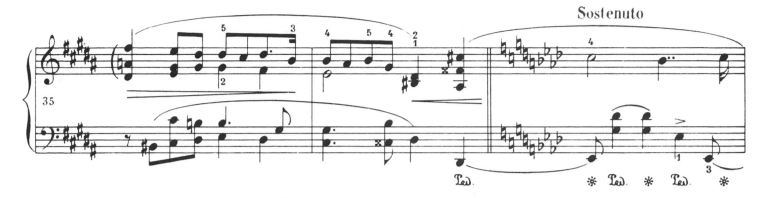

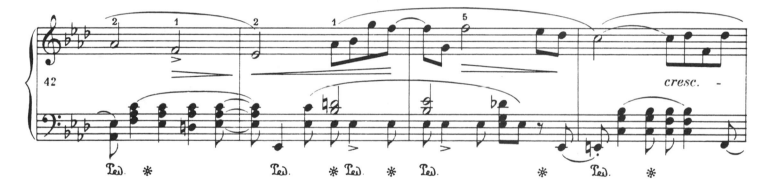

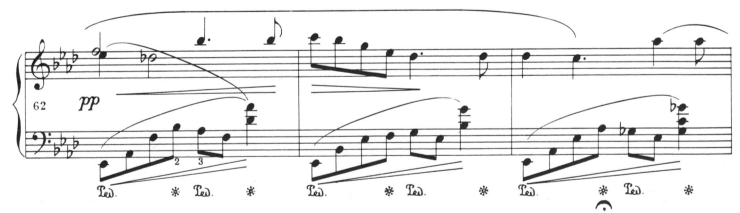

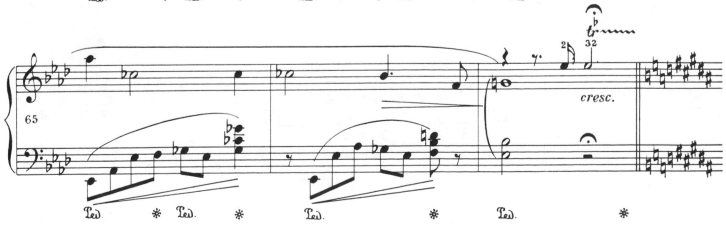

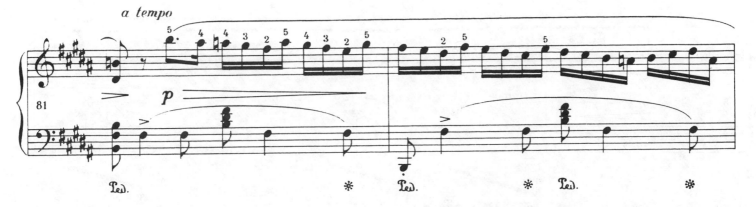

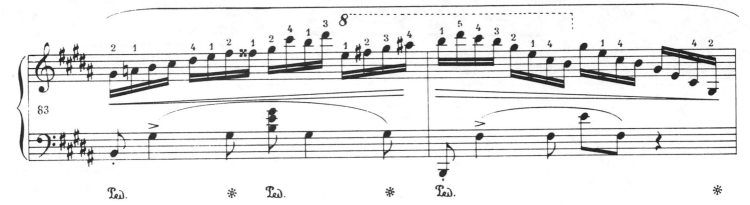

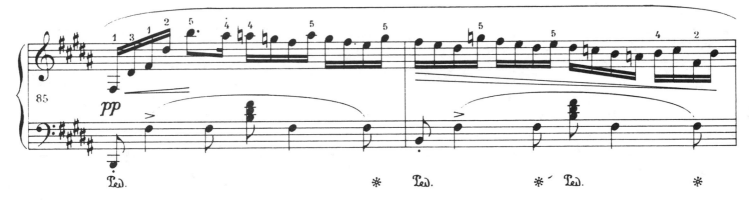

Op. 62 Nr 2

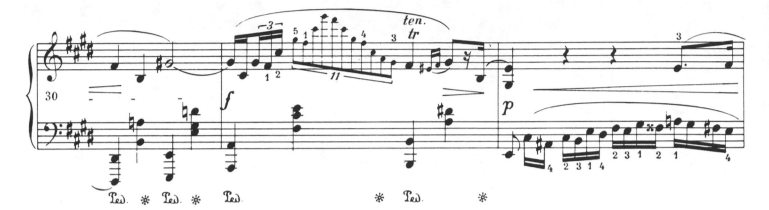

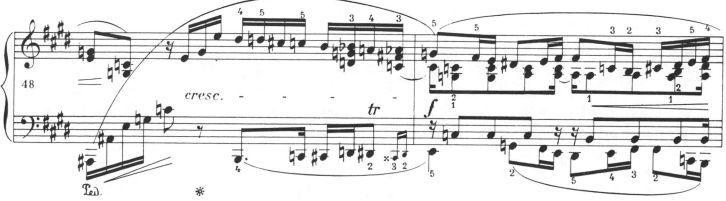

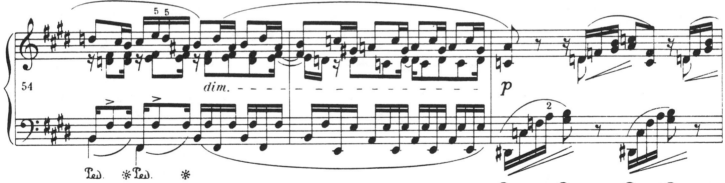

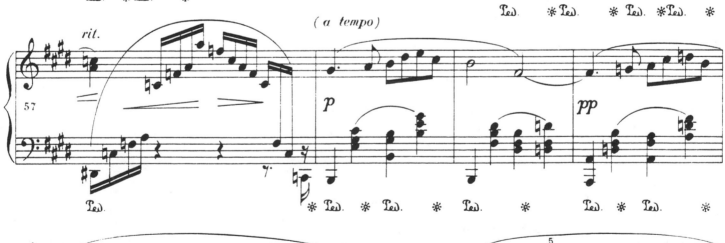

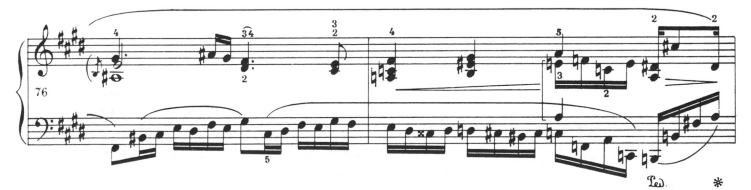

NOCTURNE

Op. 72 Nr 1
(Oeuvre posthume)

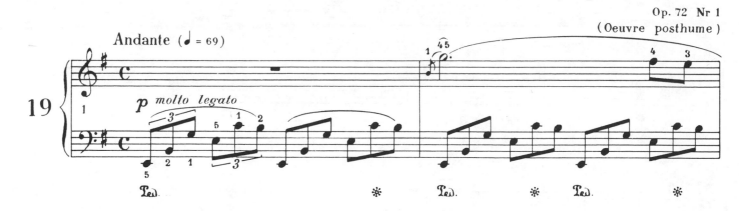

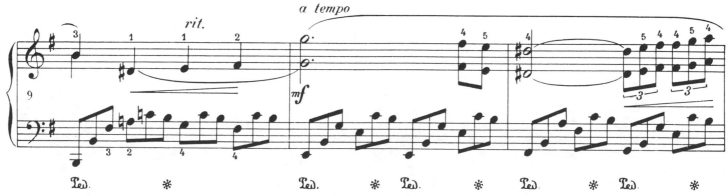

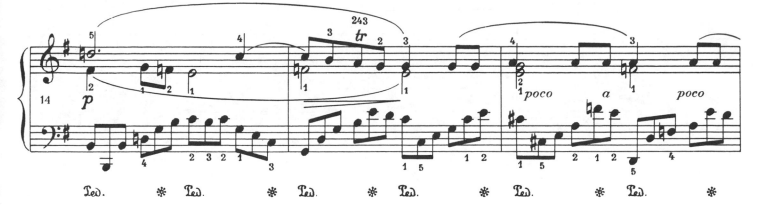

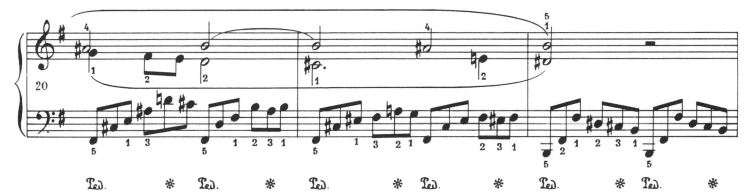

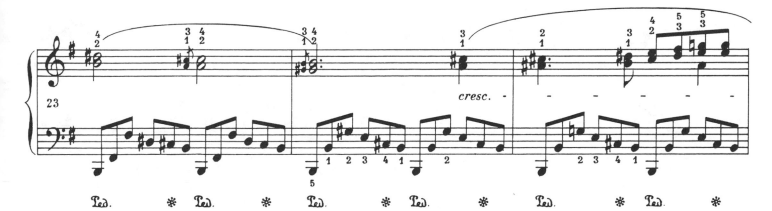

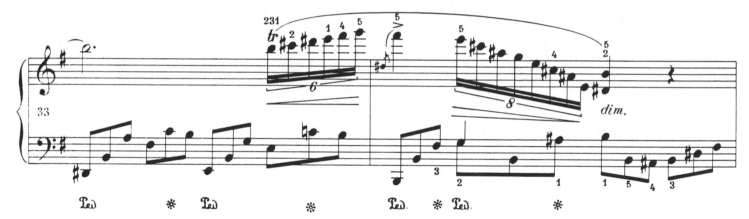

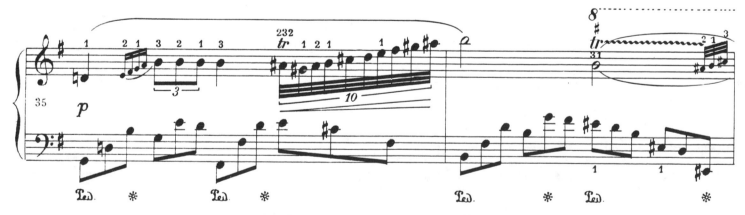

A son ami J. Dessauer

DEUX POLONAISES

FR. CHOPIN

Op. 26 Nr 1

Allegro appassionato

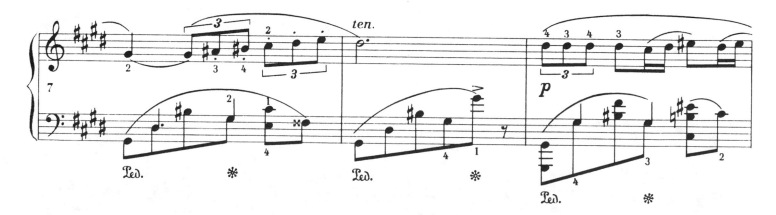

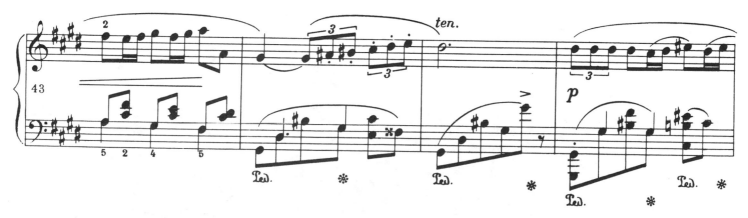

Fine

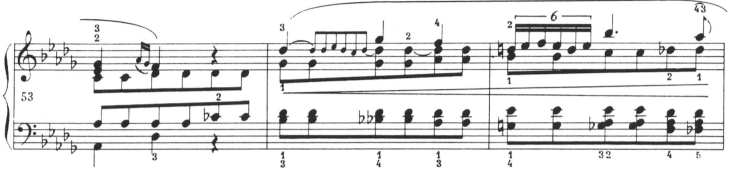

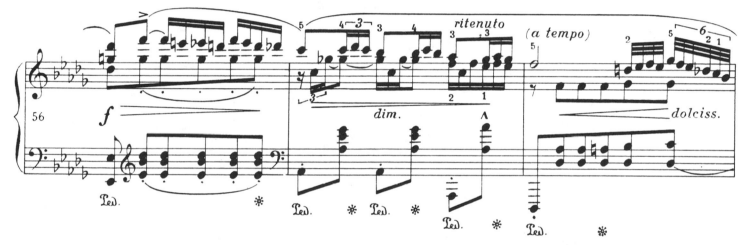

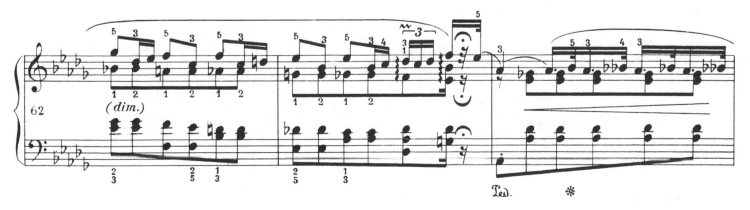

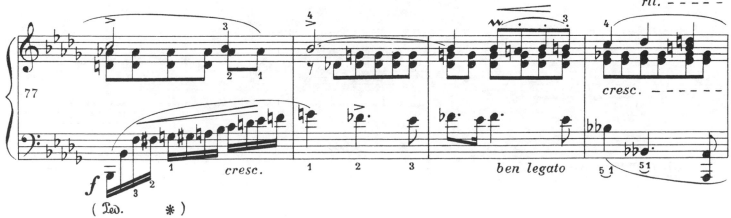

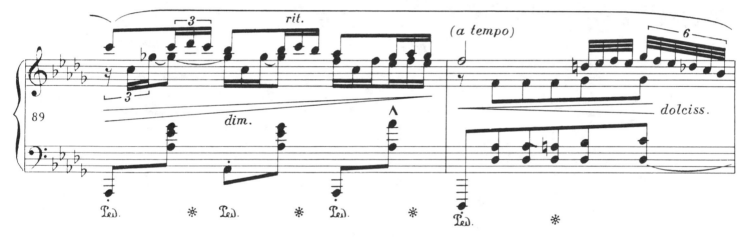

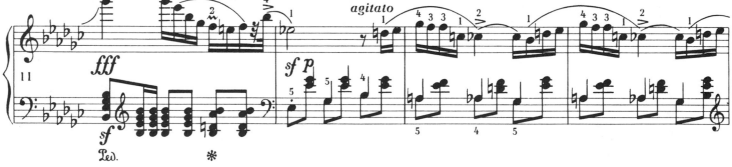

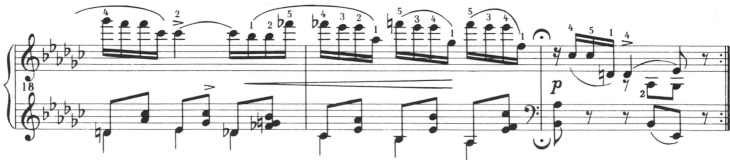

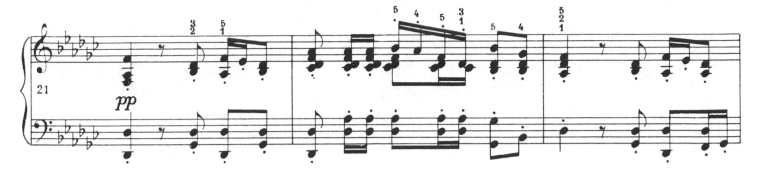

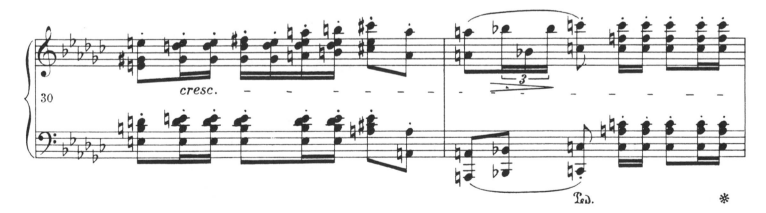

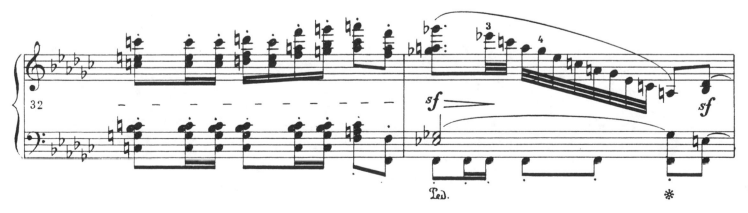

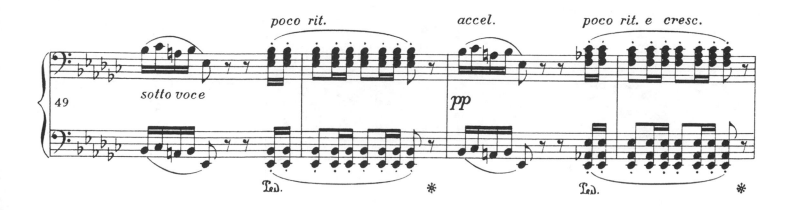

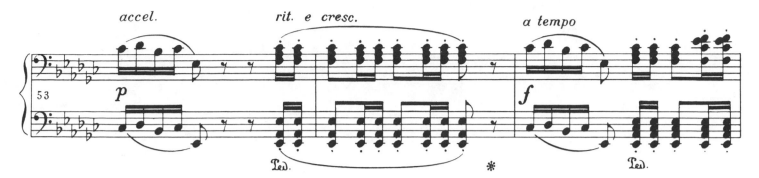

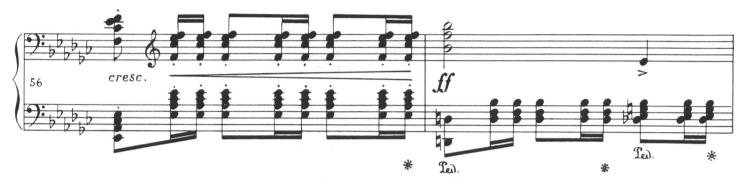

Meno mosso

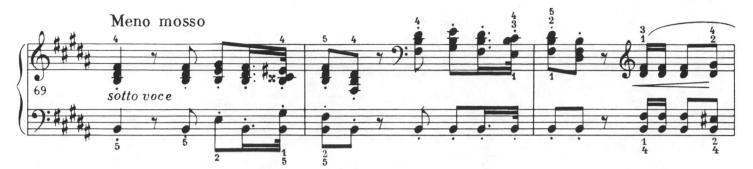

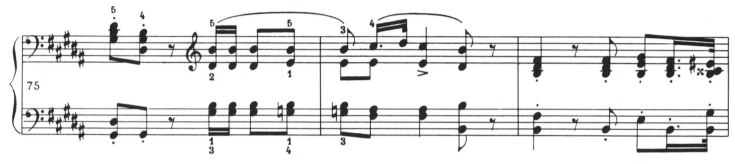

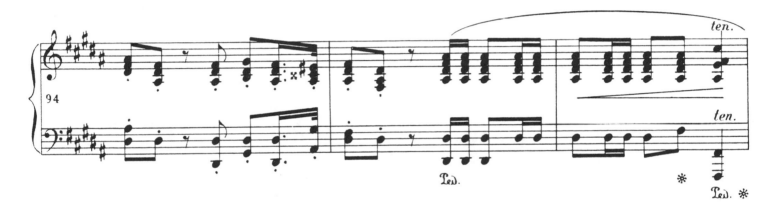

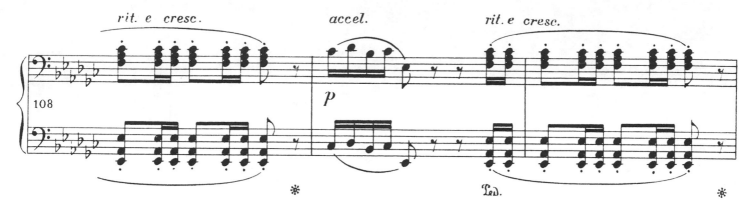

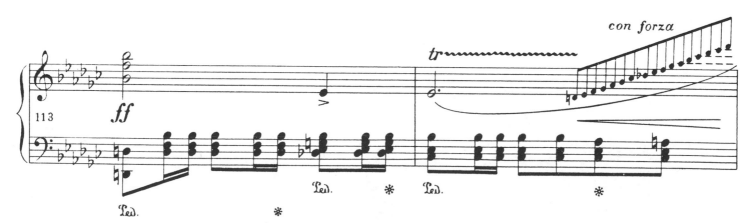

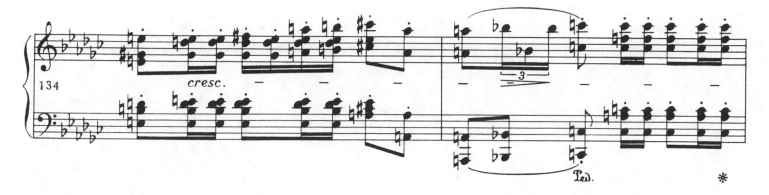

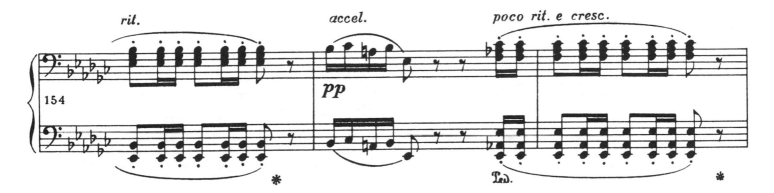

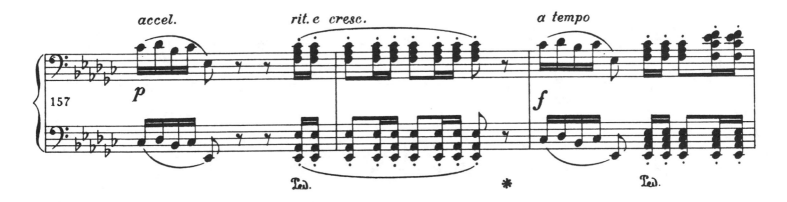

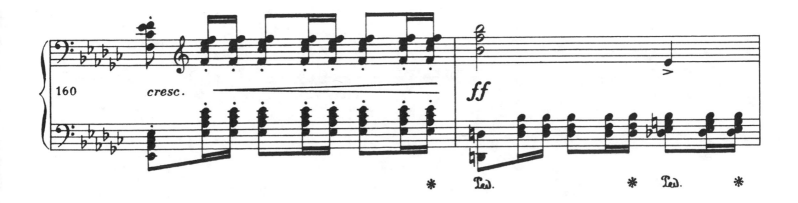

A Monsieur Jules Fontana

DEUX POLONAISES

Allegro con brio

Op. 40 Nr 1

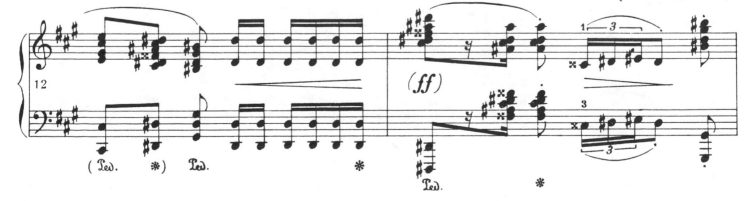

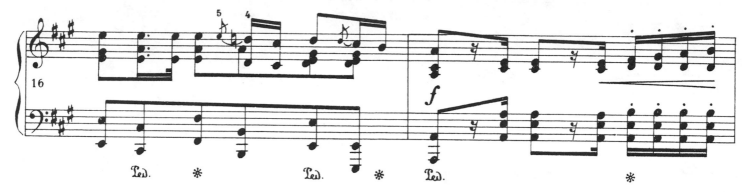

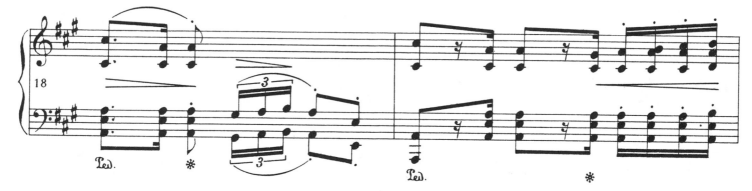

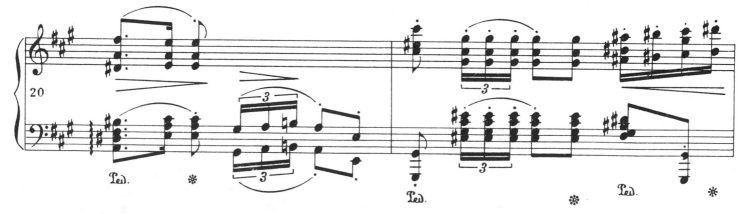

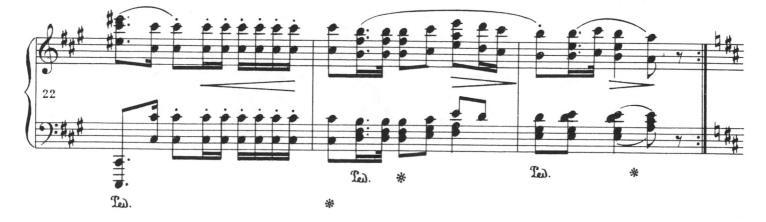

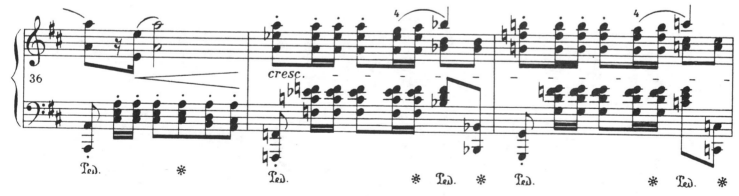

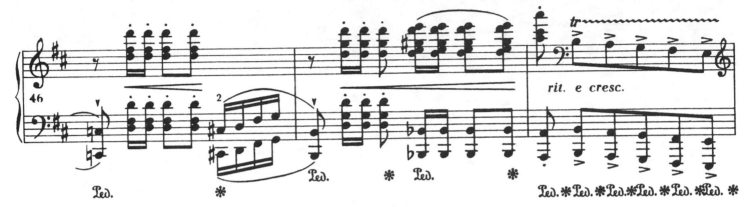

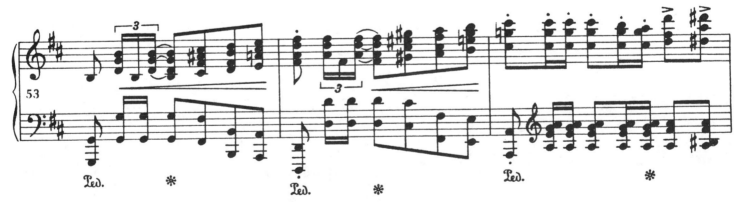

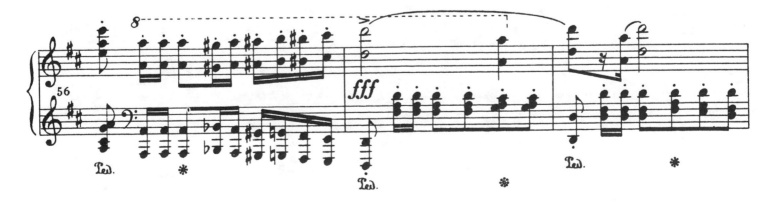

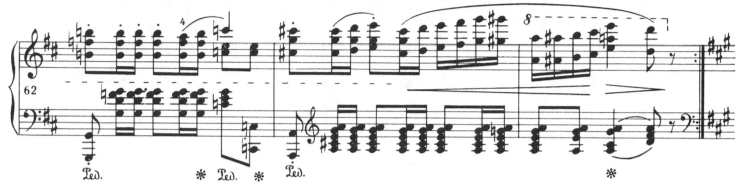

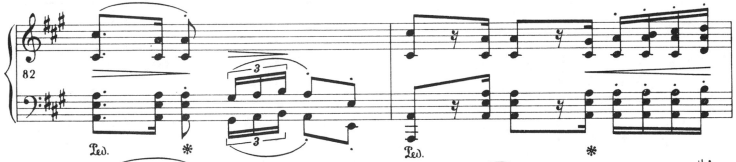

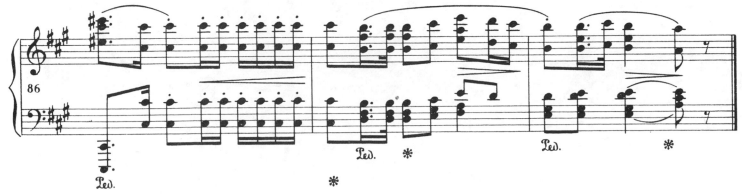

Allegro maestoso

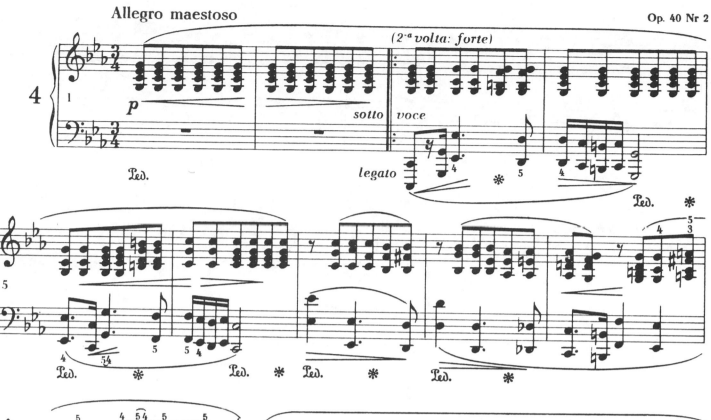

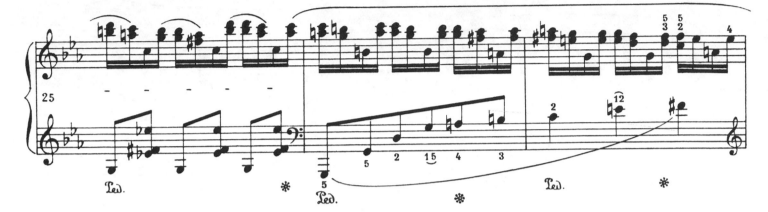

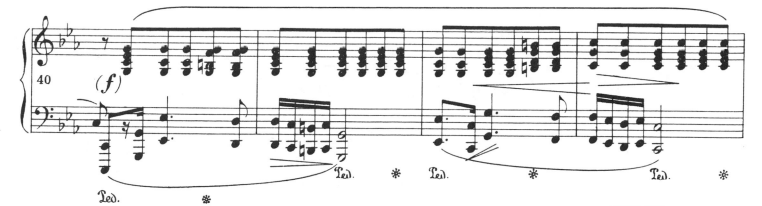

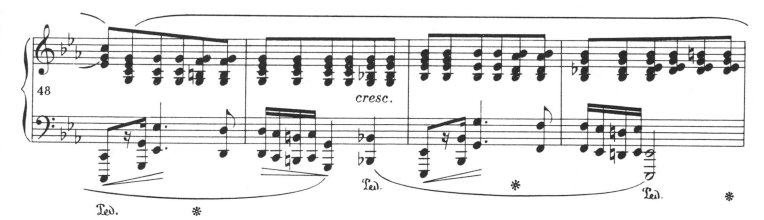

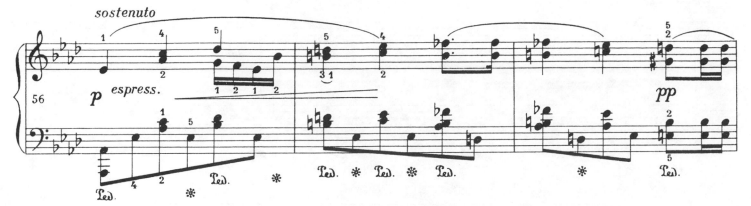

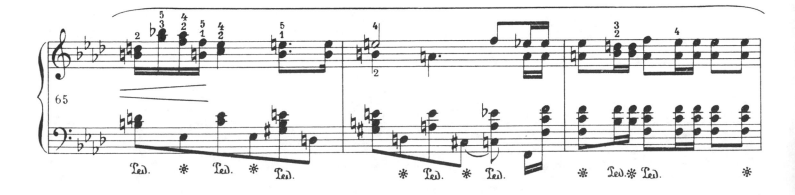

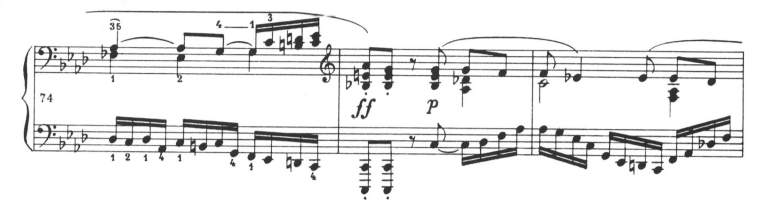

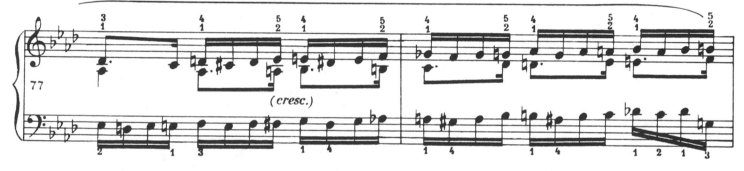

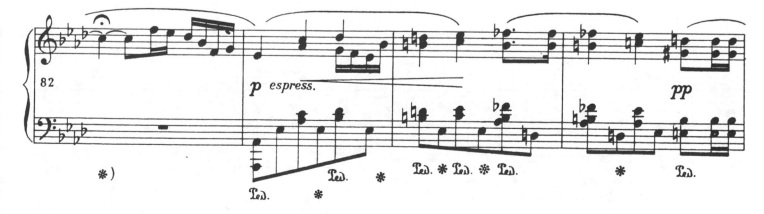

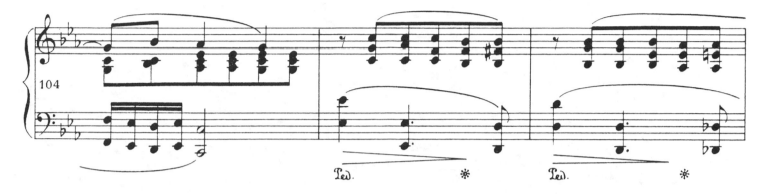

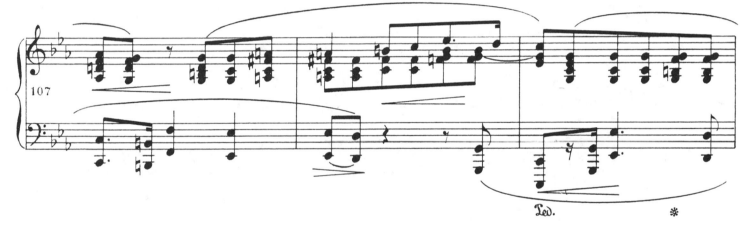

A Madame la Princesse Charles de Beauvau, née de Komar

POLONAISE

Op. 44

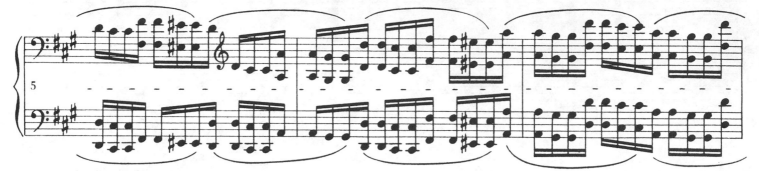

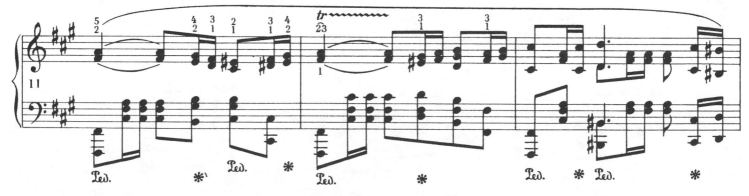

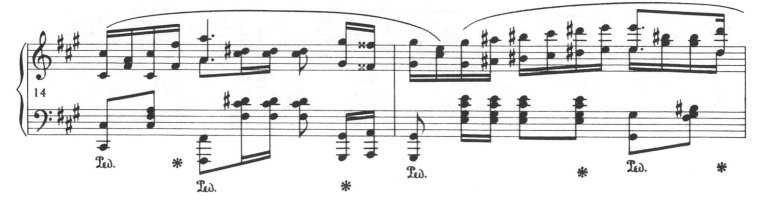

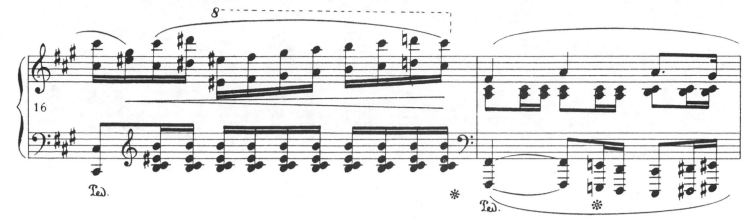

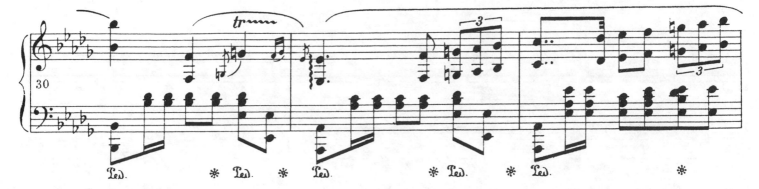

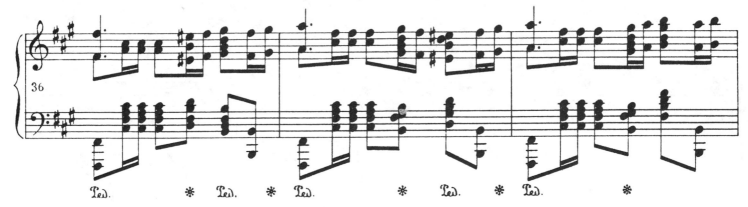

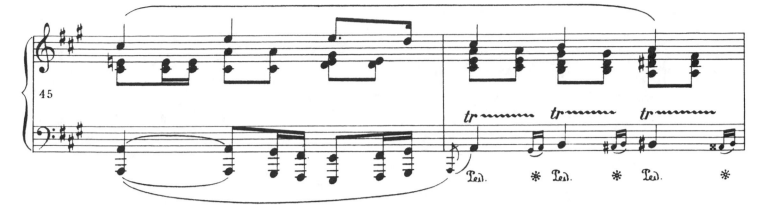

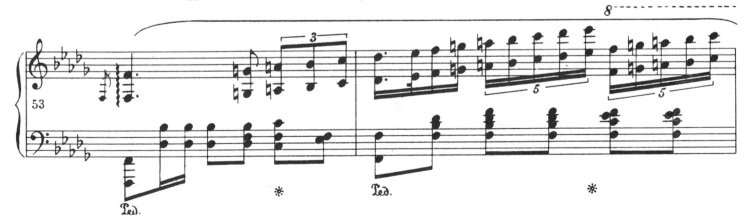

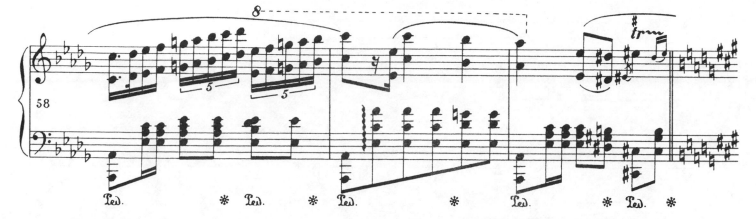

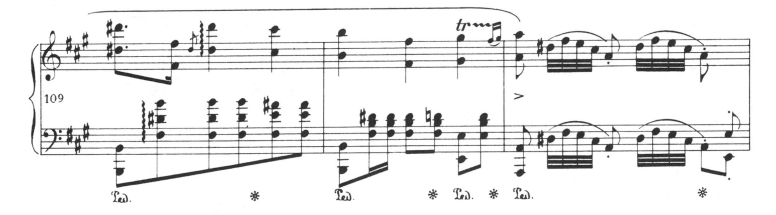

Doppio movimento (Tempo di Mazurka)

sotto voce

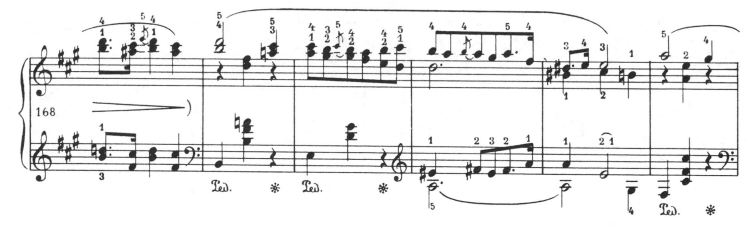

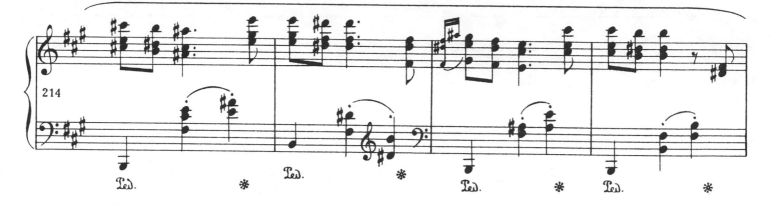

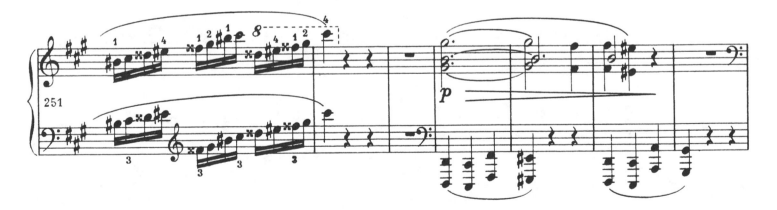

Tempo I (tempo di Polacca)

262

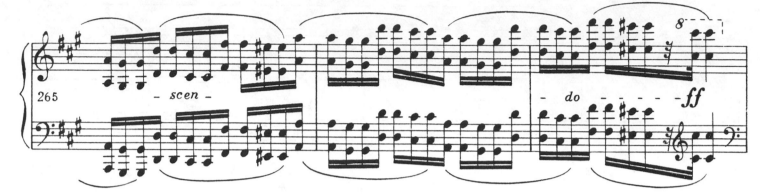

265

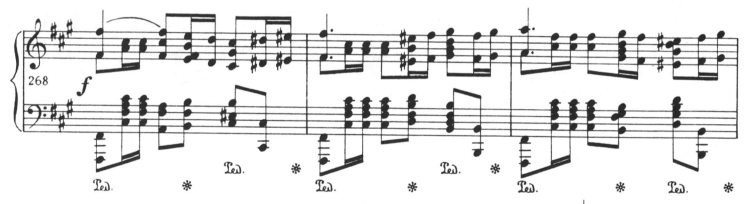

268

271

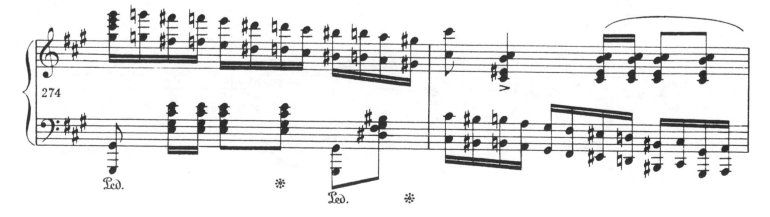

274

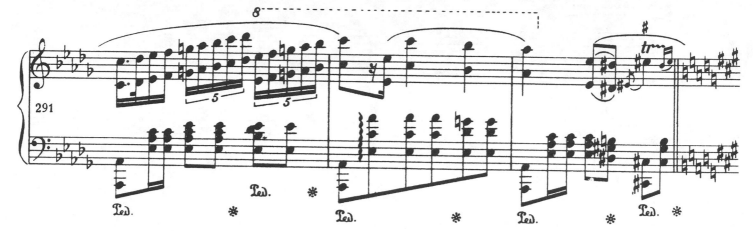

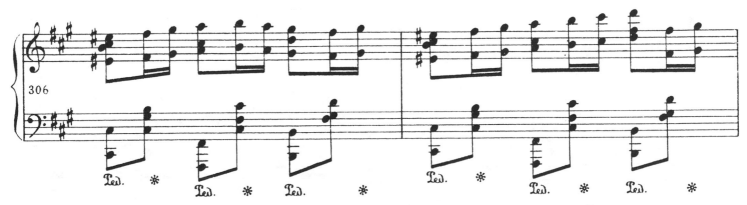

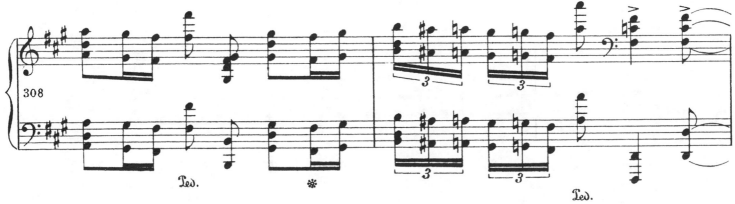

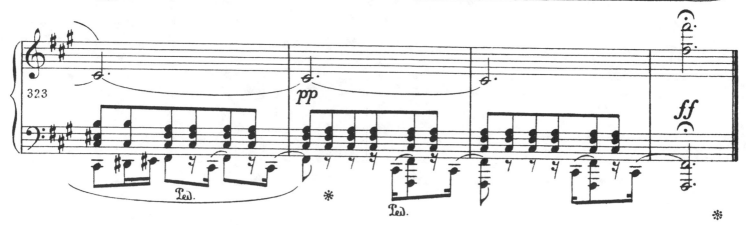

A Monsieur Auguste Léo

POLONAISE

Op. 53

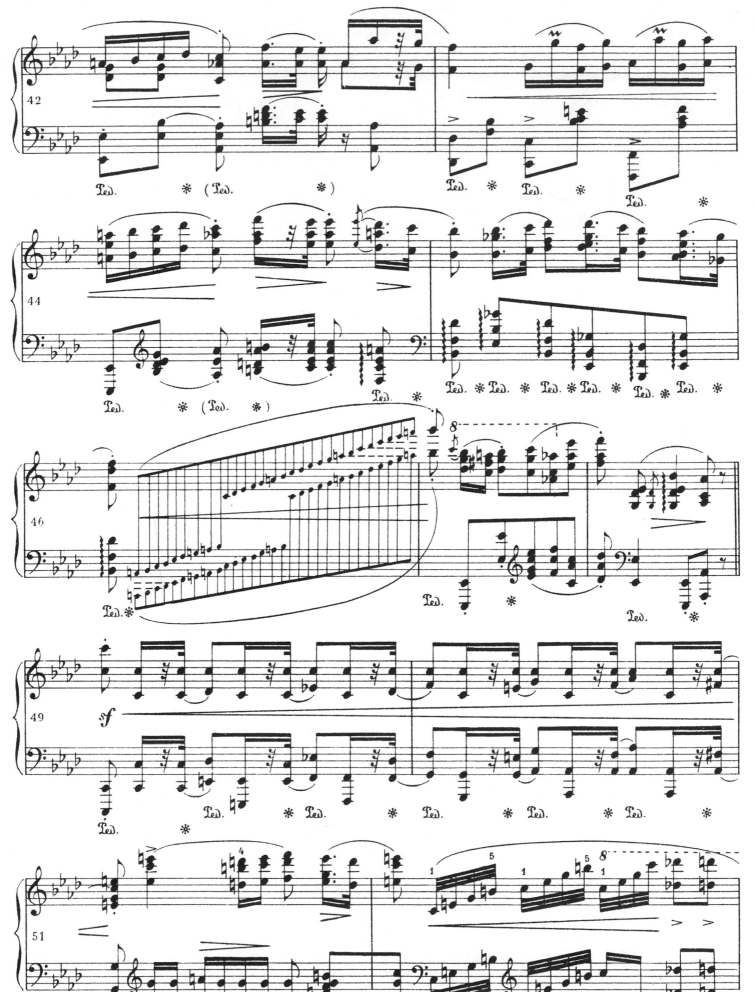

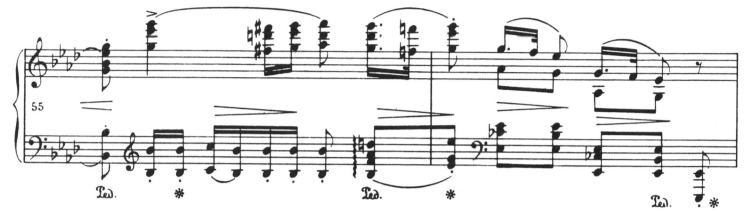

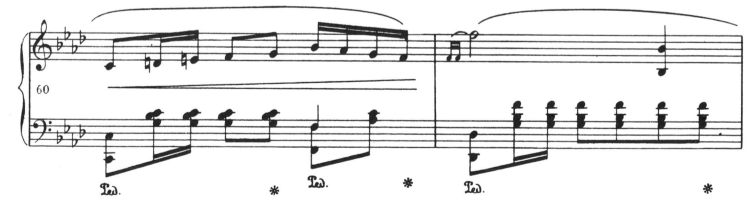

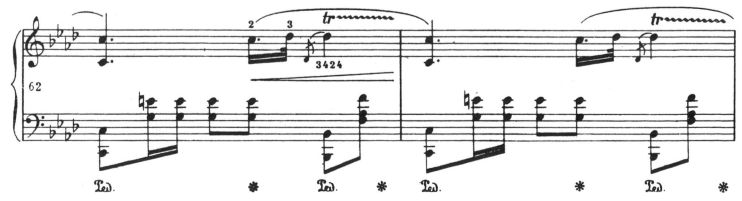

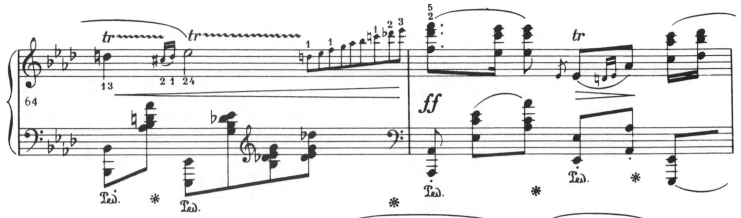

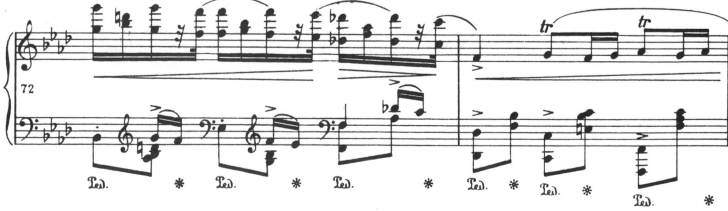

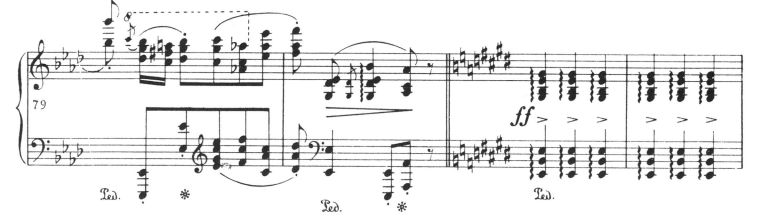

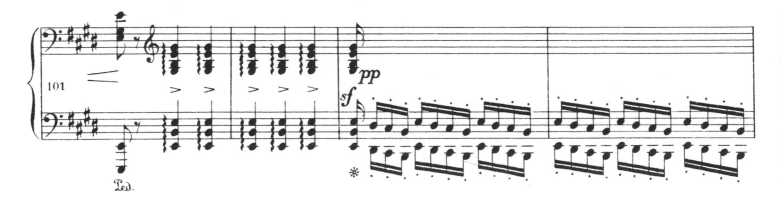

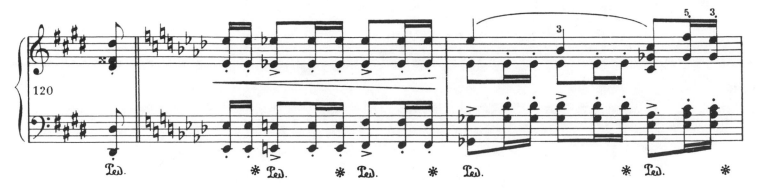

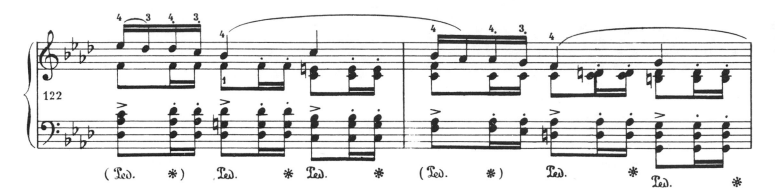

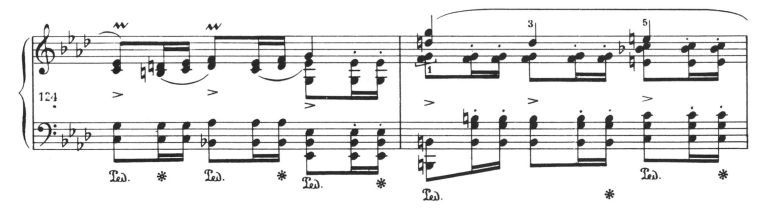

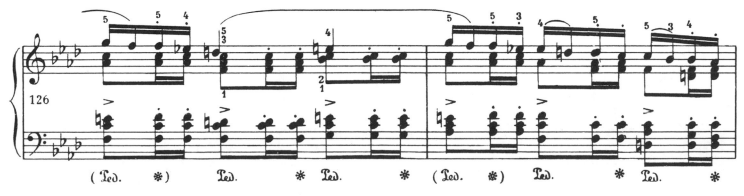

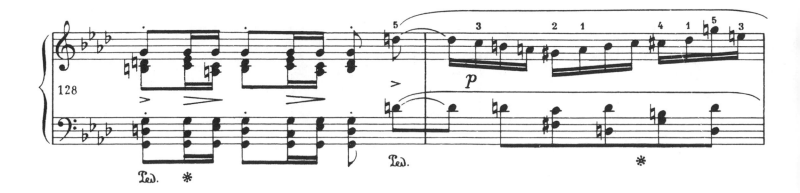

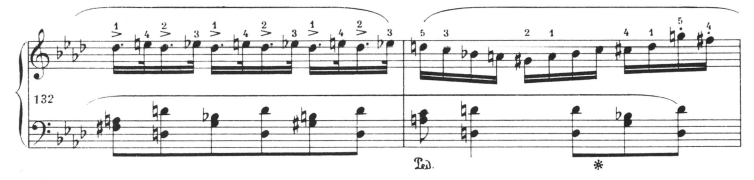

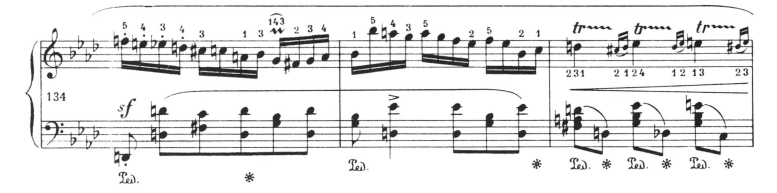

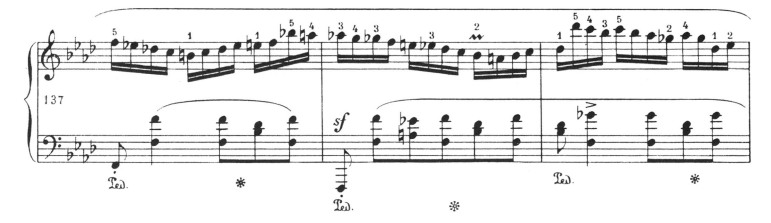

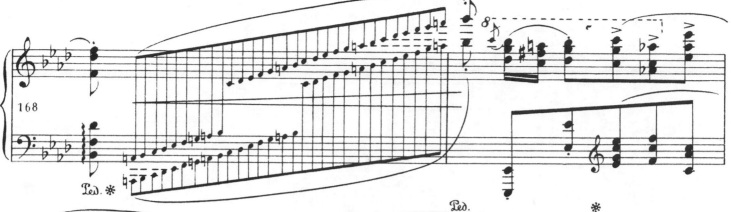

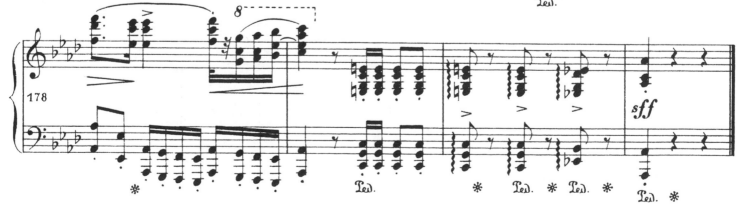

A Madame A. Veyret

POLONAISE–FANTAISIE

Op. 61

Allegro maestoso

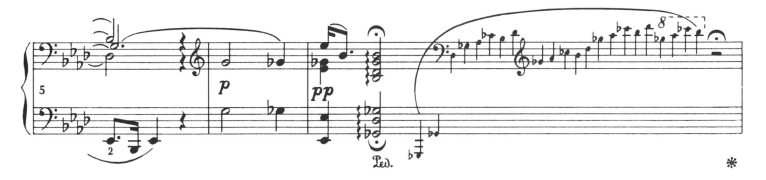

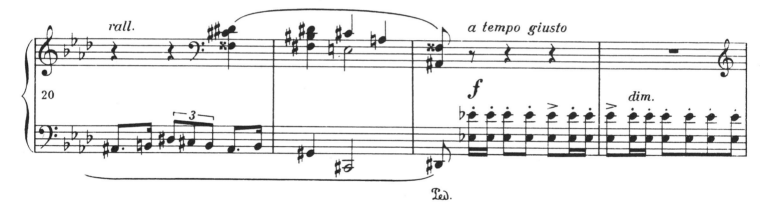

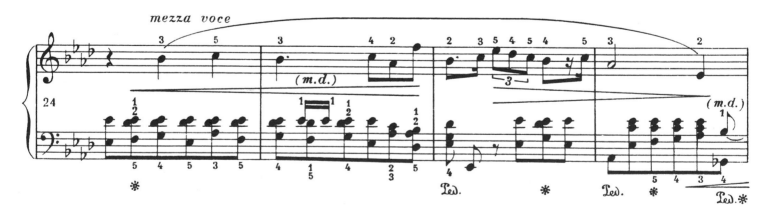

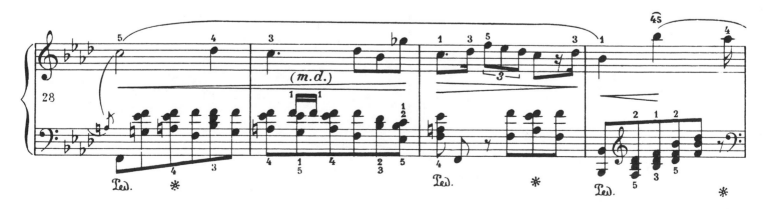

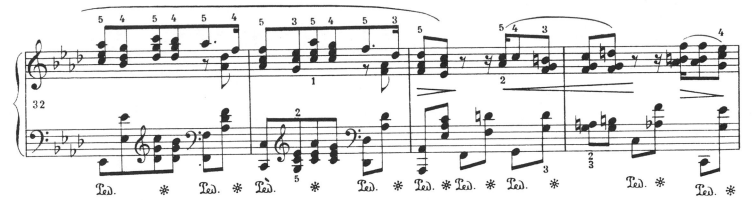

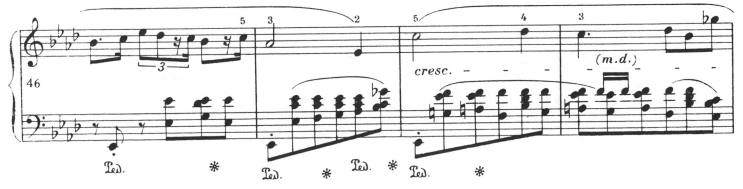

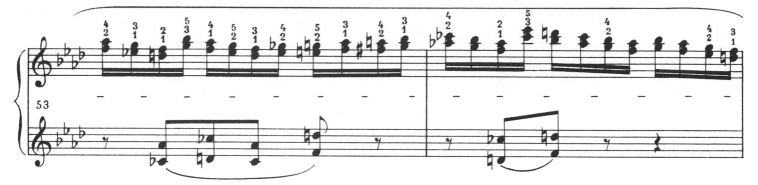

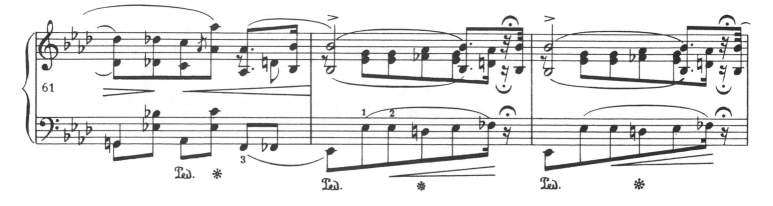

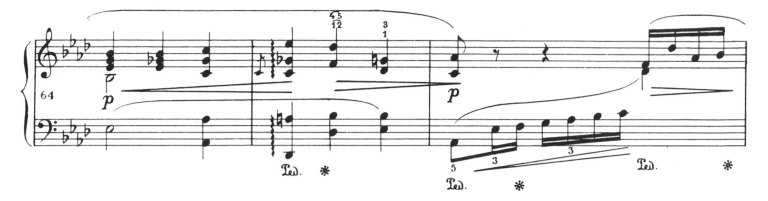

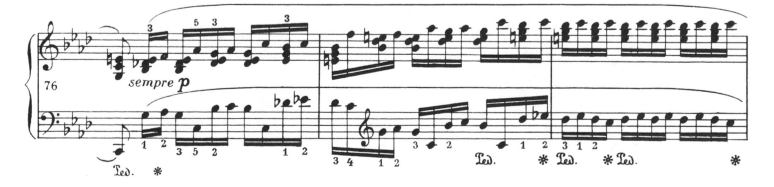

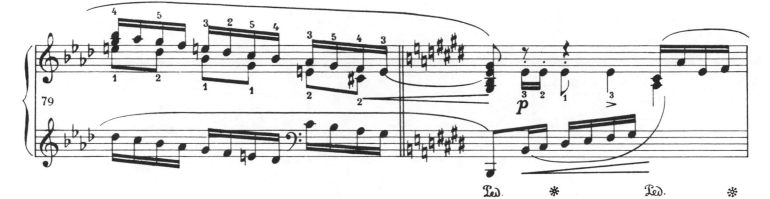

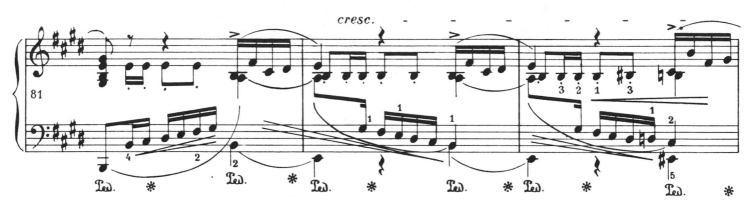

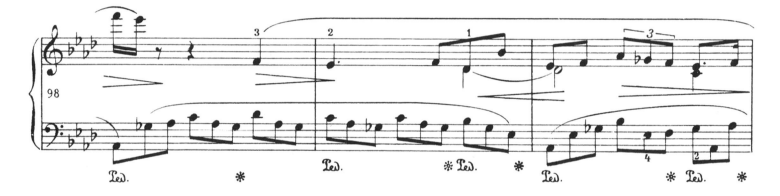

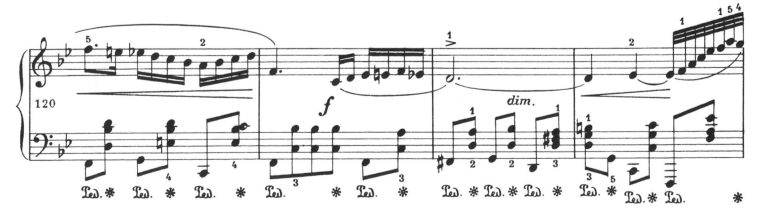

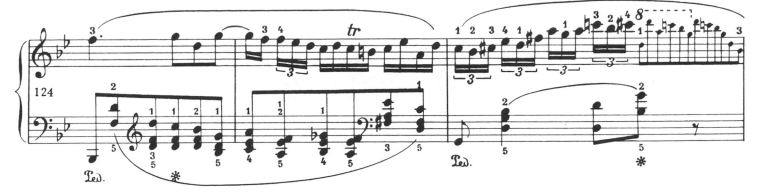

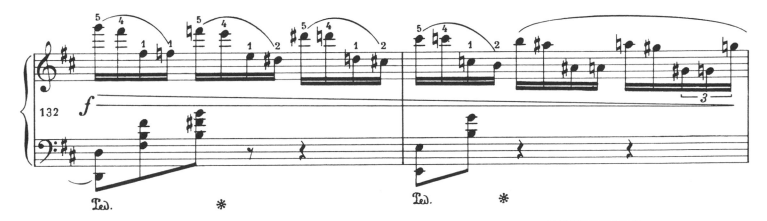

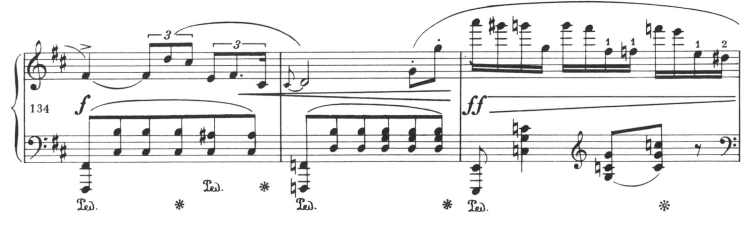

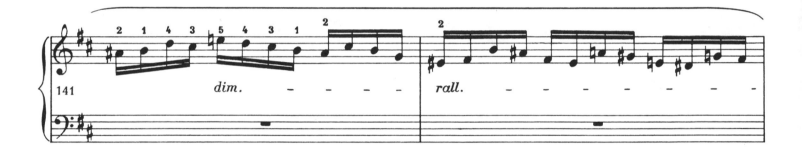

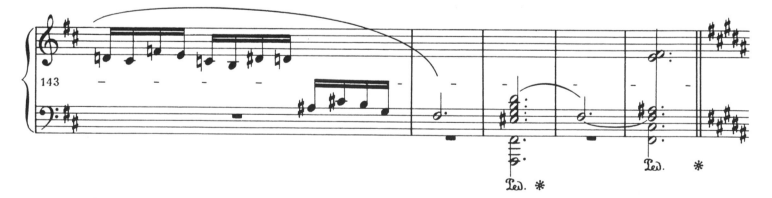

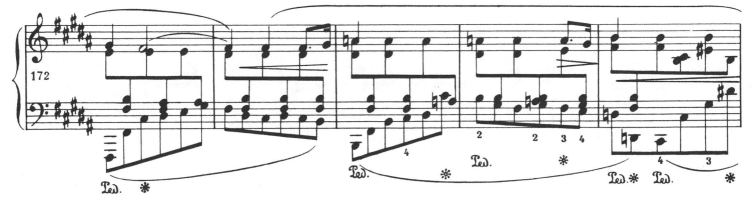

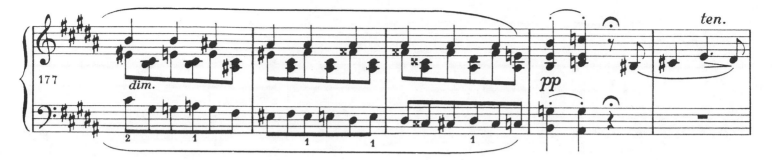

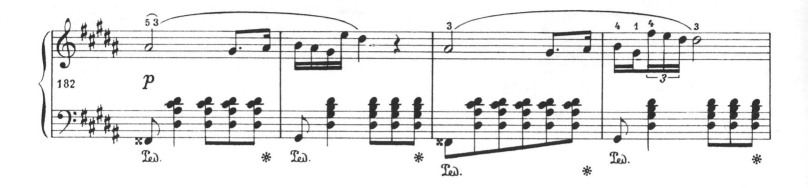

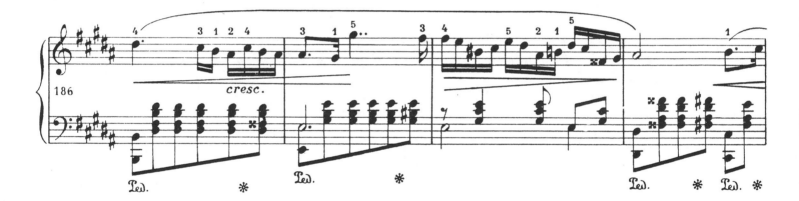

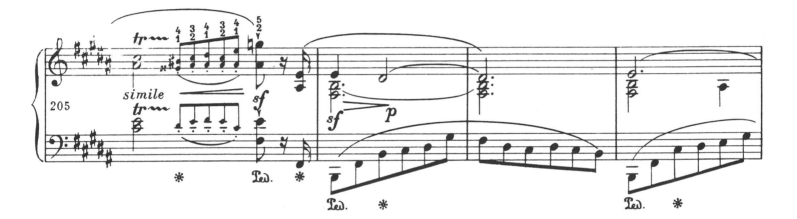

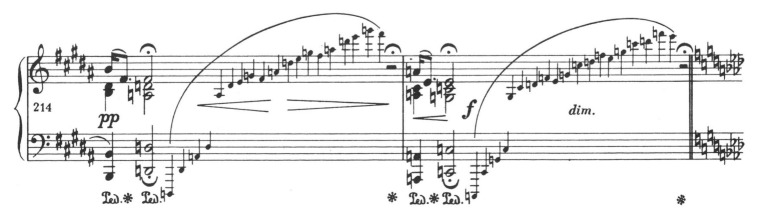

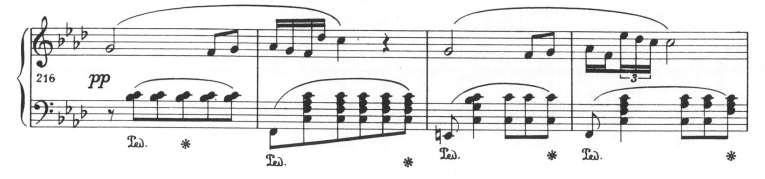

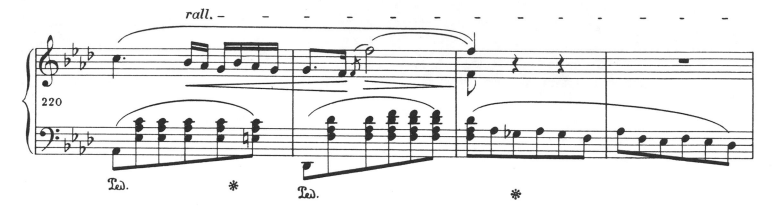

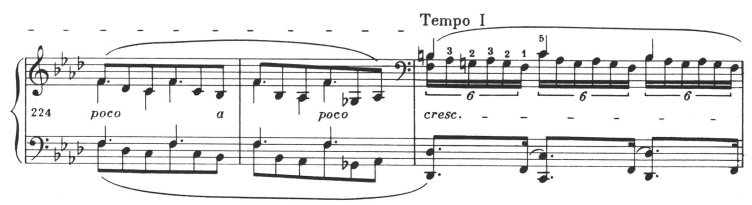

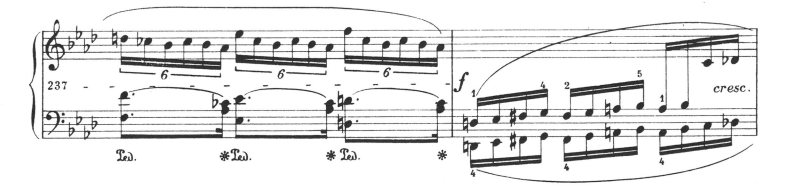

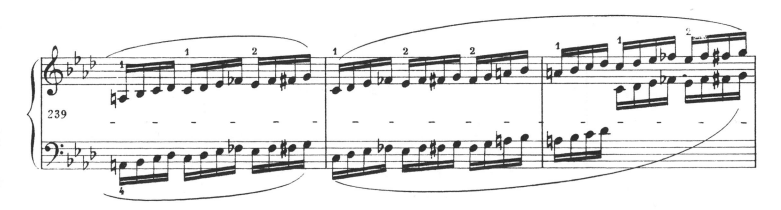

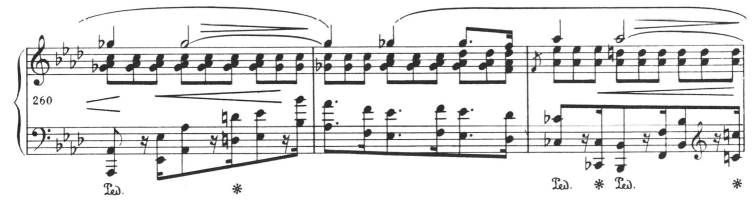

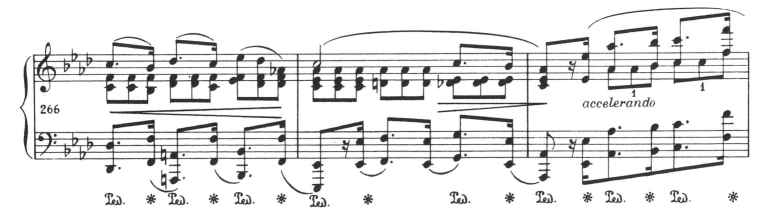

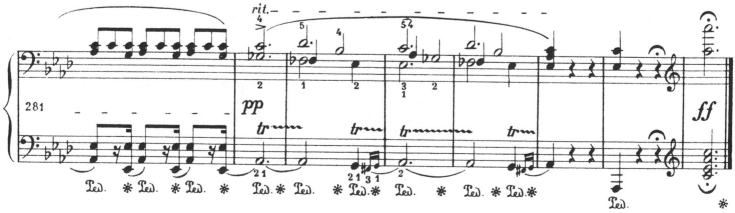

TROIS POLONAISES

(Oeuvres posthumes)

Op. 71 Nr 1

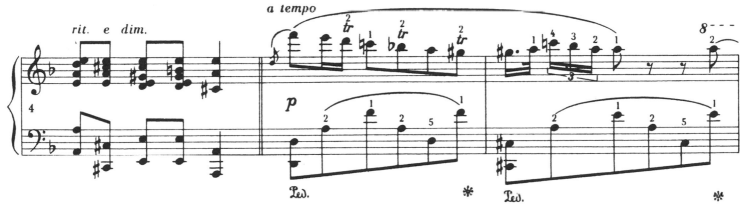

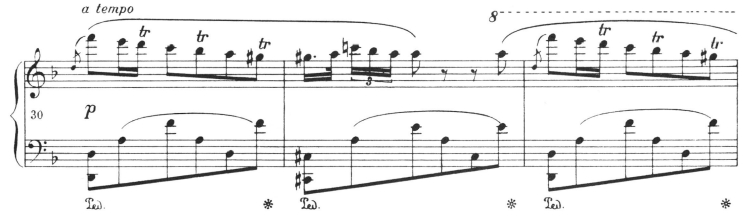

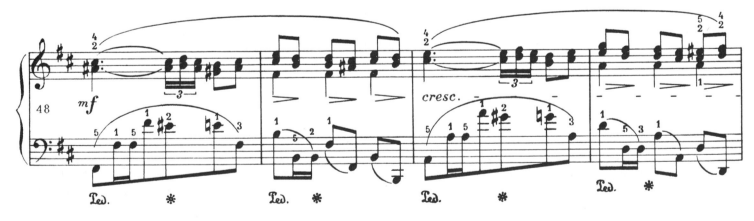

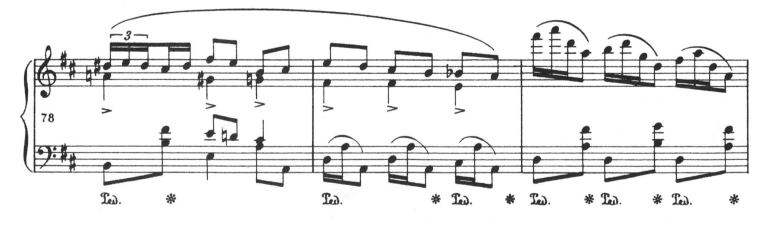

D.C.senza repetizione sin' al Fine

Allegro, ma non troppo ♩ = 92

risoluto

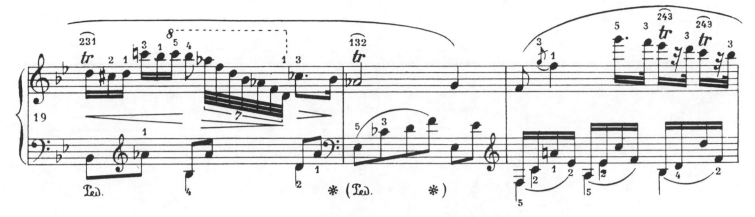

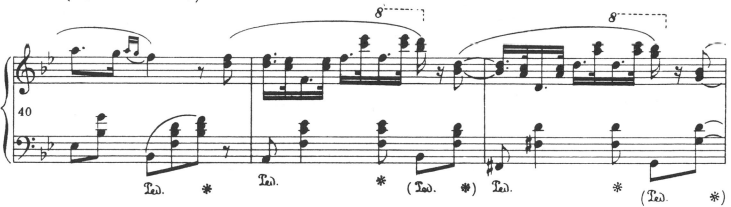

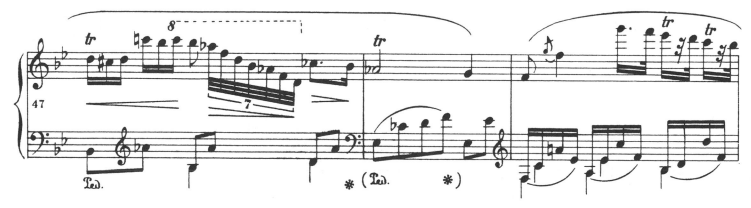

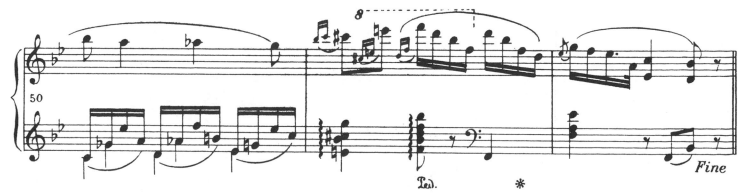

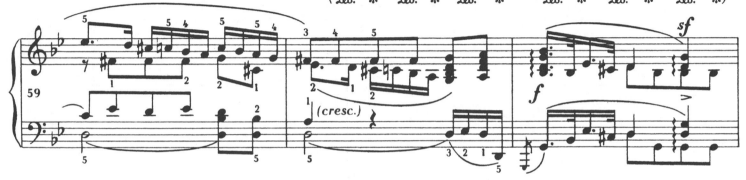

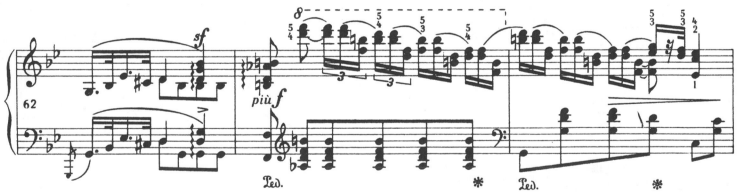

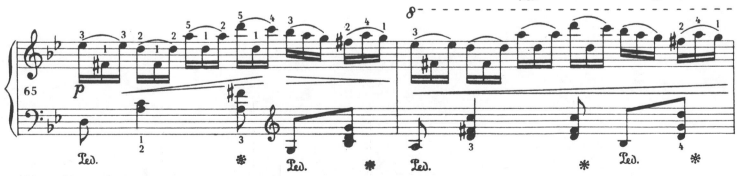

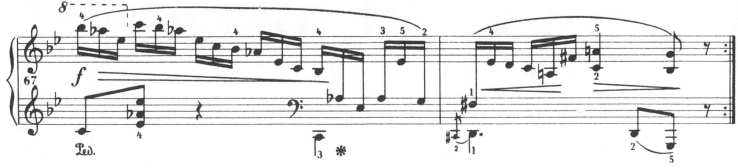

192

D. C. senza repetizione sin' al Fine

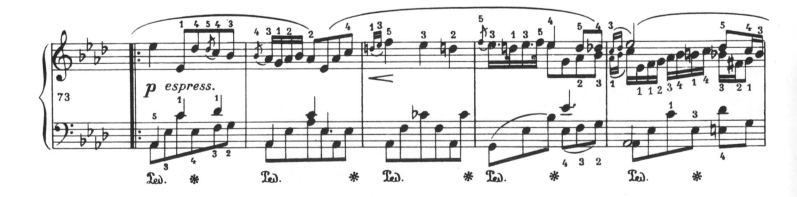

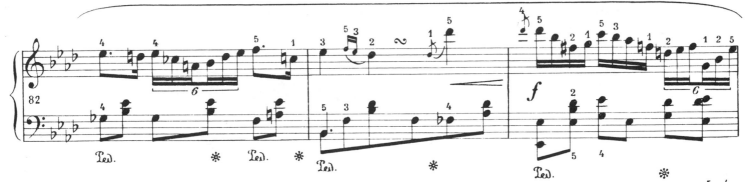

D.C. senza repetizione sin' al Fine

Dédiée à Son Excellence Mme la Comtesse Victoire Skarbek

POLONAISE

[Allegro, ma non troppo]

(Oeuvre posthume)

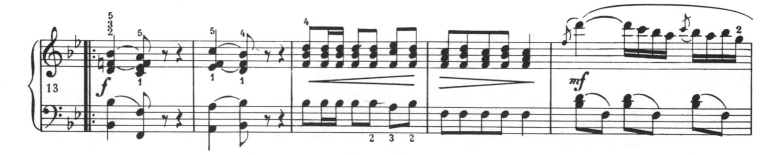

TRIO

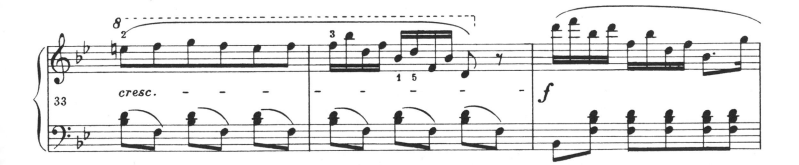

Polonaise da capo al Fine

POLONAISE

(Oeuvre posthume)

TRIO

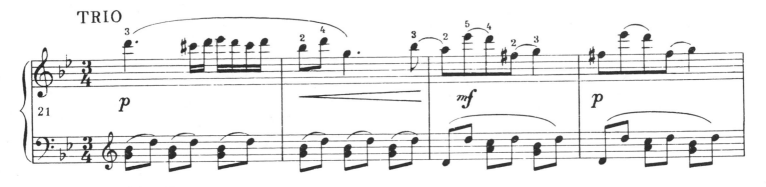

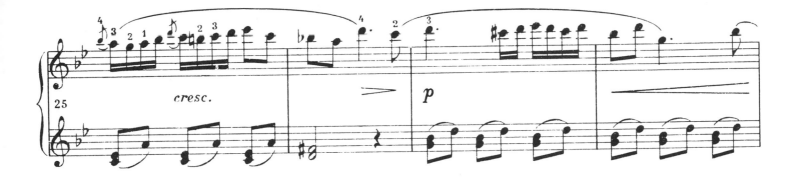

Polonaise da capo al Fine

POLONAISE

(Oeuvre posthume)

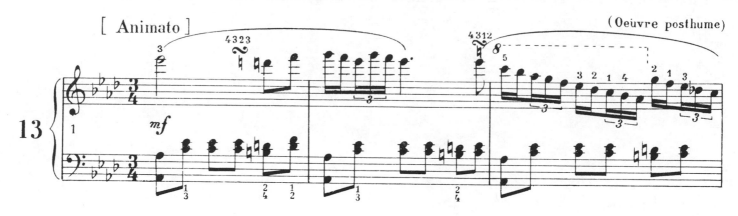

TRIO

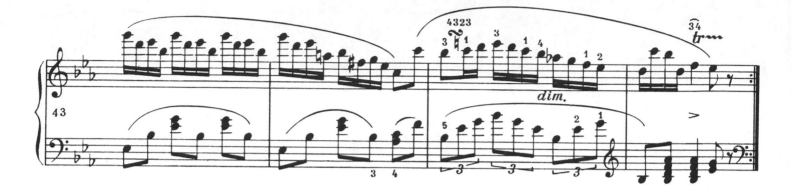

Polonaise da capo al Fine

POLONAISE

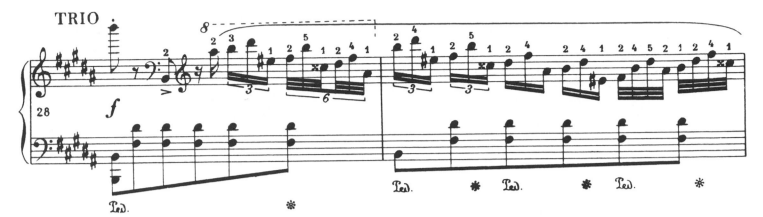

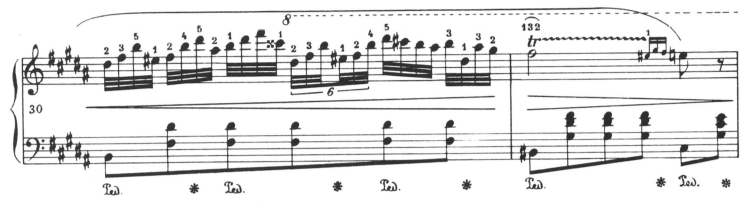

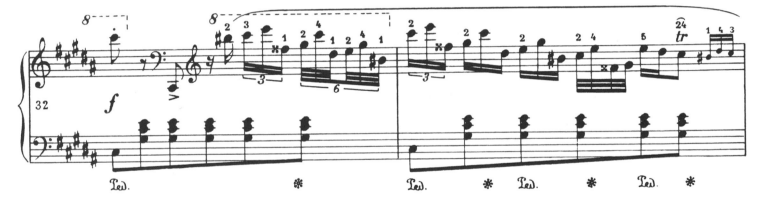

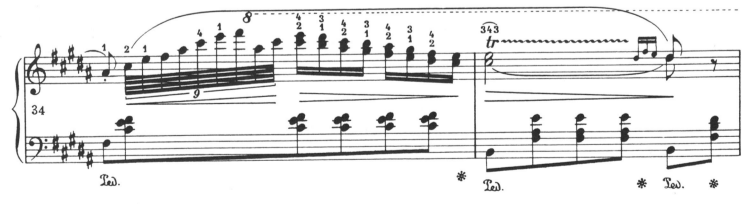

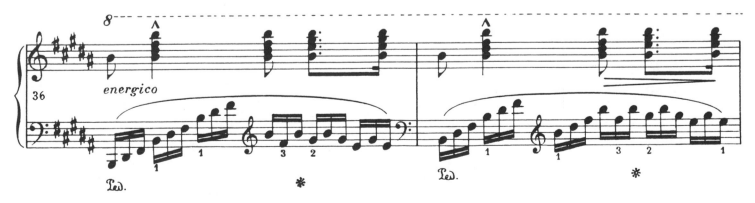

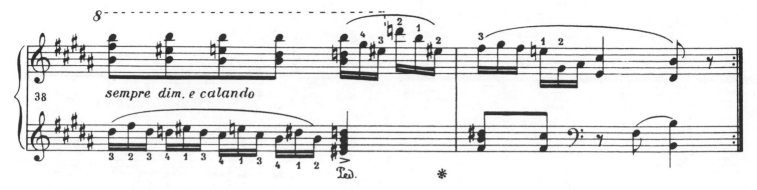

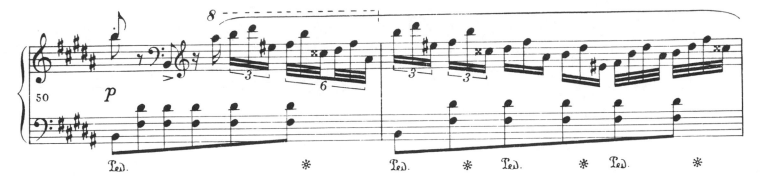

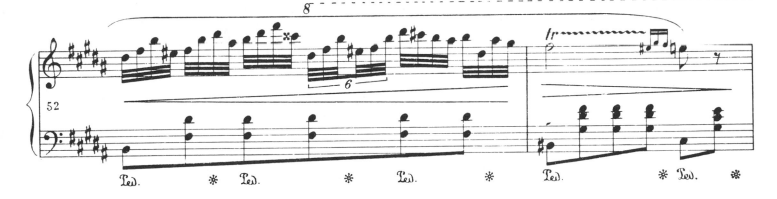

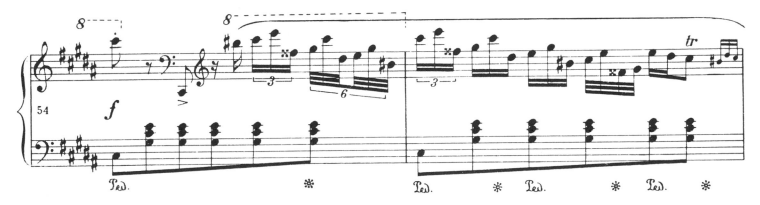

Polonaise da capo al Fine

A Guillaume Kolberg

Adieu!

POLONAISE

[Allegro moderato]

(Oeuvre posthume)

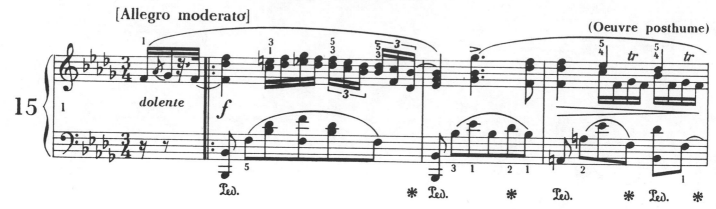

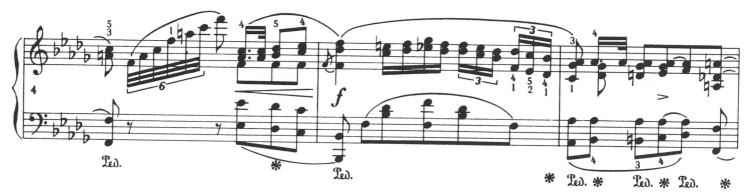

TRIO

Do widzenia! (według arii z opery „ Sroka złodziej" Rossiniego) *Au revoir!* (D'après un air de «La Gazza ladra»)

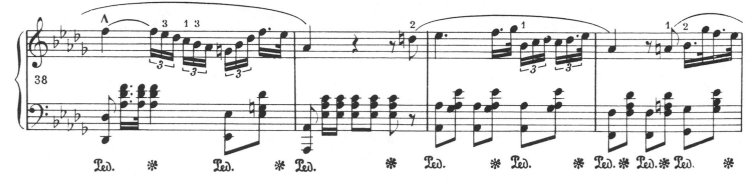

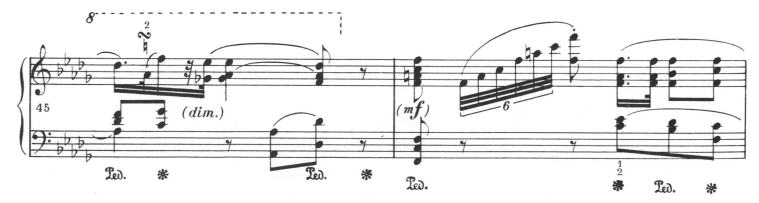

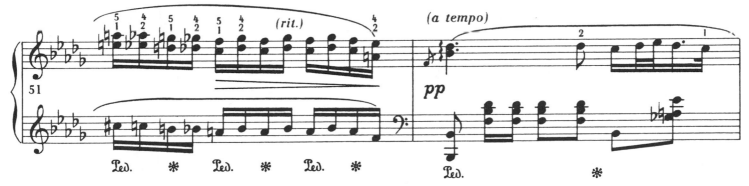

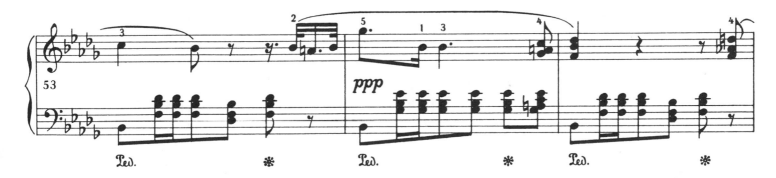

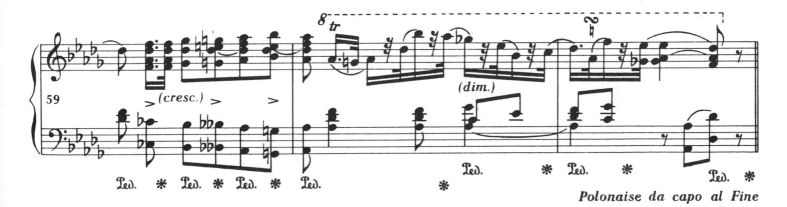

Polonaise da capo al Fine

POLONAISE

[Maestoso]

(Oeuvre posthume)

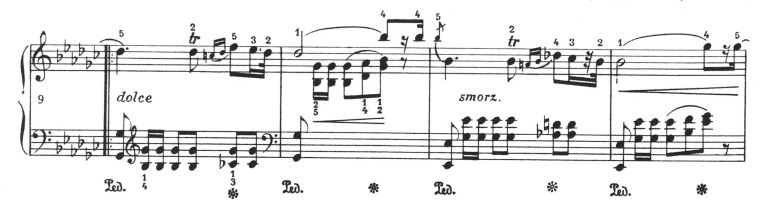

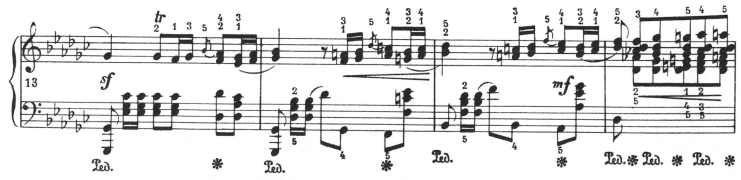

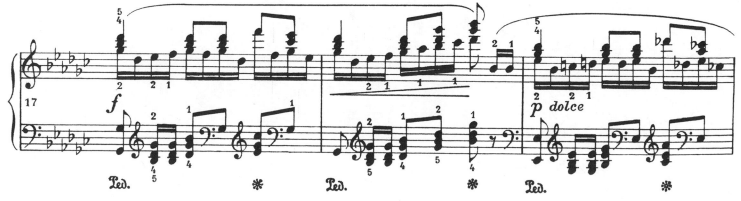

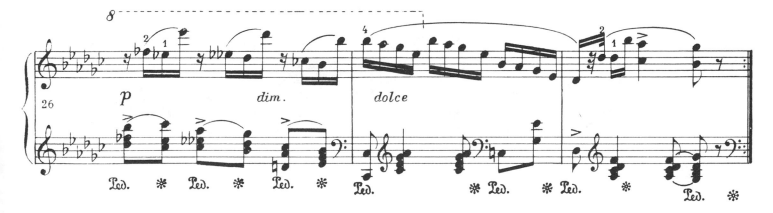

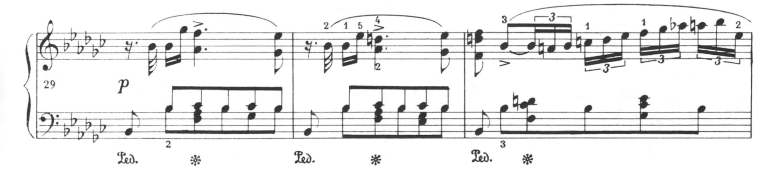

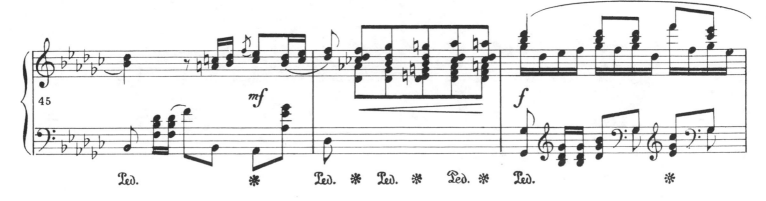

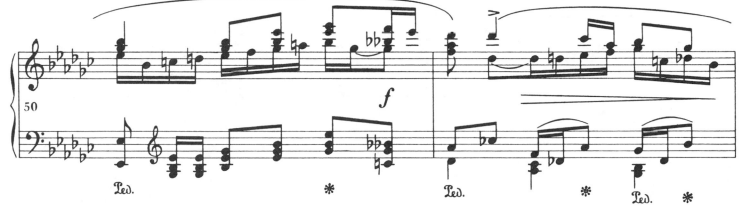

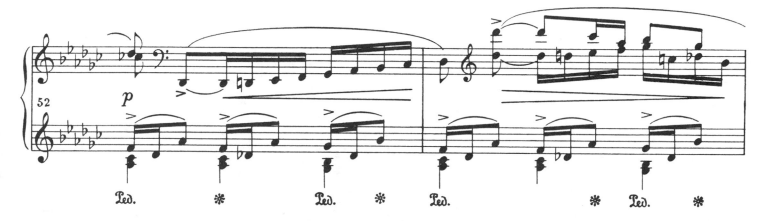

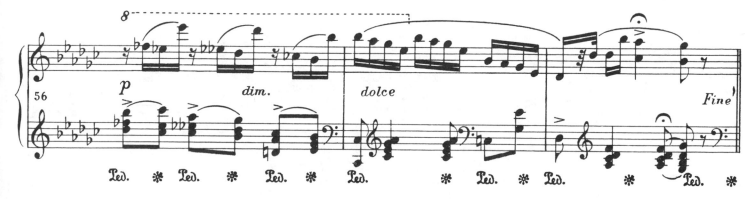

TRIO

Meno mosso

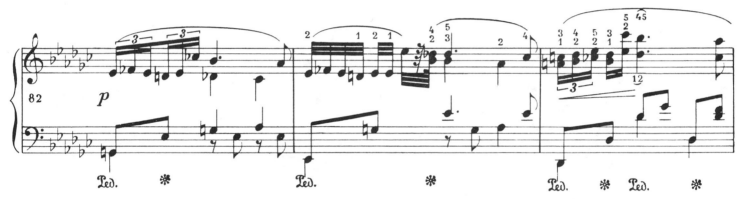

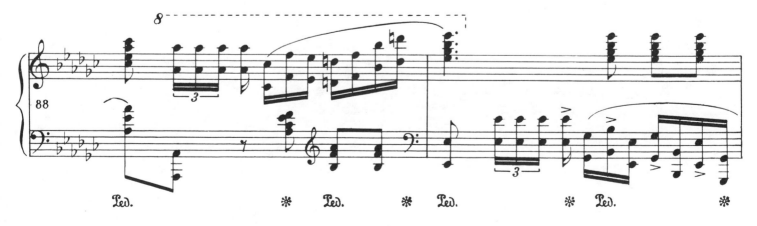

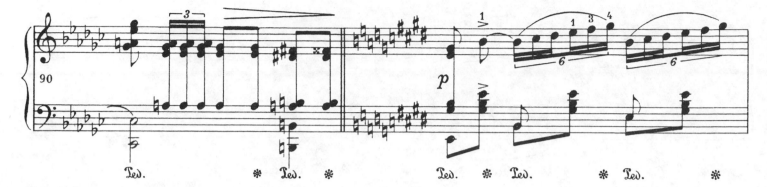

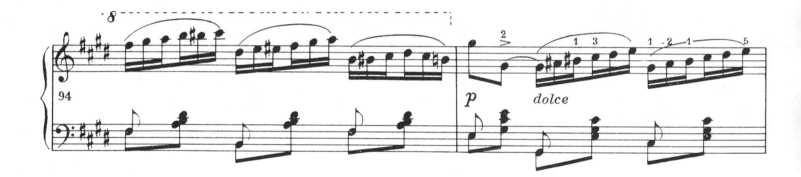

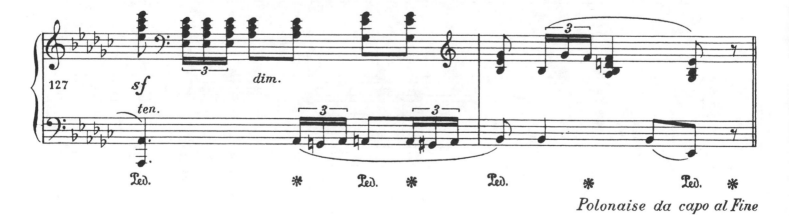

Polonaise da capo al Fine

THE CHARACTER OF THE PRESENT EDITION

The principal aim of the Editorial Committee has been to establish a text which fully reveals Chopin's thought and corresponds to his intentions as closely as possible. For this reason the present edition has been based primarily on Chopin's autograph manuscripts, copies approved by him and first editions. The Committee has had to take into account the fact that even though a manuscript may have served as a basis for a first edition, it is not always the final version of any particular piece. Chopin frequently changed details of his compositions up to the very last moment. So much is clear not only from contemporary sources, but also from variants between original editions and manuscripts. Such variants, moreover, cannot possibly be considered to be engraver's errors or editorial alterations. The manuscripts will always be the prime source for the textual verification of Chopin's works. But although no effort has been spared, it has not always been possible to discover or study a given manuscript. The Editorial Committee has also consulted recent editions for purposes of comparison.

When it has proved impossible to establish the authentic version or the one corresponding to Chopin's last intentions, any discrepancy has been carefully indicated in the Commentary.

Dynamic and agogic signs correspond to the manuscripts and first editions. Sometimes they have been supplemented by the repetition of signs appearing in identical or similar places. Other additions have been placed in brackets. Chopin's original fingering, rare though it is in the manuscripts and first editions, has been expressly indicated in the Commentary.

The pedal marks given by the Editorial Committee are strictly in accordance with the manuscripts and original editions. Certain insignificant modifications have been introduced, but only where this is required by the greater resonance of modern pianos, as well as in analogous passages or repetitions, where comparison has revealed inconsistency, or where correction or completion is required owing to mistakes or negligence. Chopin's pedal-marking is usually careful, precise, and in certain places very delicate, sometimes producing entirely new pianistic effects (e.g. at the beginning of the Polonaise-Fantasia). Those passages in which Chopin has not marked the pedalling are generally explained by the fact that the pedalling required is very simple, and is therefore self-evident; or, on the contrary, that it is so subtle as to be too complicated, if not impossible, to indicate. In any case, the use of the pedal is a very delicate and entirely individual matter, depending on many factors, such as instrument, touch, tempo or acoustics of the room. For this reason, the Editorial Committee has decided to leave the pedalling as found in the original documents. This conforms with the principles adopted in the present edition.

In principle, Chopin's phrasing has been retained. But certain slurs have been modified in the interests of simplicity, exactitude or clarity. In Chopin's manuscripts slurs are sometimes placed carelessly, and do not always correspond in original editions.

The editors have introduced some slight modifications of the original in the arrangement and outward appearance of the musical text. Harmonic notation and accidental signs have been altered or added where necessary, and certain changes in the distribution of notes have been effected so as to ensure the clearest visual presentation of the music, of the composer's intentions, and to safeguard the performer from hesitations, uncertainties or misunderstandings. In these cases, the editors have endeavoured to keep to the notation of the manuscripts and first editions as closely as possible, and have tried to avoid the exaggerations which sometimes characterize previous editions of Chopin's works.

For this reason also, we have very often left certain inconsistencies occurring in the notation of similar passages undisturbed. Such variants often appear in Chopin's works, not only in the notation but also in the contents of the music. Any important modification of Chopin's notation, however, has been clearly indicated in the Commentary.

In ornamentation, Chopin's original notation has been retained; attention has been drawn to any ornament appearing in different forms in the manuscripts and original editions. Wherever the execution of an ornament may give rise to doubt, the most appropriate manner has been carefully shown.

The chief difficulty lies in the method of beginning a trill. The following principles should be observed:

1) Where the principal note of a trill is preceded by an upper appoggiatura: , or by a sequence of grace notes: , the trill begins on the upper note:

In the latter case ( ), the repetition of the principal note at the beginning should be avoided.

The following: does not exist in Chopin. To obviate this mistake certain editors have added an upper appoggiatura to the notation of these trills:

2) Where the principal note of the trill is preceded by the same note written as an appoggiatura: , the trill should always begin on the principal

note: but should never be played thus:

 etc.

3) Doubt may arise where the notation of the trill contains no appoggiatura. In his study *Ornamentation in the Works of F. Chopin* (London 1921, p. 1), J. P. Dunn suggests that in these cases the trill should always begin on the principal note (as if it were

written:).

Contrary to the opinion often expressed that a trill should always begin on the upper note, this principle is confirmed by the fact that Chopin sometimes writes a trill with an appoggiatura on the same pitch level as the principal note, and at other times, in a similar or corresponding place, completely omits the appoggiatura, and *vice-versa*; e. g. in the autograph of the first movement of the Sonata in B minor the trill in bar 52 is written without an appoggiatura, while the corresponding trill in the recapitulation has, in addition to the principal note, an appoggiatura on the same pitch level. There is no reason whatsoever to suppose that the second trill should be executed differently from the first.

Dunn adds (op. cit., p. 24) that the trills written without the principal note given as an appoggiatura may sometimes begin on the upper note, where this does not disturb the melodic line. Generally speaking, it can be established as a principle that in doubtful cases the trill should be started so as to link up as smoothly as possible with the preceding notes, e. g. filling a missing step or avoiding the repetition of a principal note, already performed (cf. ex. 1 and 2).

4) Difficulty may arise from the fact that Chopin sometimes used *tr* in place of the conventional sign to indicate a mordent. In the autograph MS of the Ballade

in A♭ major a simple mordent sign appears in bar 3, while at the corresponding point in bar 39 Chopin has written *tr* (see also Bronisława Wójcik-Keuprulian *Melodyka Chopina*, Lwów 1930, p. 56). This is justifiable in so far as the mordent is a short form of the trill, and in a quick movement the trill is often executed as a mordent. Places where the *tr* sign may be taken to be a mordent have been indicated in the Commentary.

5) When the ending of a trill is not expressly indicated, the trill should always be completed by playing the principal note after the upper note.

6) Finally, it must be remembered that all ornaments, whether appoggiaturas, mordents, trills, turns or arpeggios, should be performed according to the accepted principle, i. e. the duration of the ornament must be subtracted from the duration of the principal

note, e. g.:   is played:

 or

In Chopin's works, the signs written in his own hand in the copies of Madame Dubois, now preserved in the Library of the Paris Conservatoire (see E. Ganche *Dans le souvenir de Fr. Chopin*, Paris 1925, p. 205 et seq.), leave no doubt, from the rhythmic point of view, as to Chopin's method of executing these ornaments. There, *inter alia*, we find signs indicating that the first note of the ornament in the upper staff is to be played simultaneously with the bass note corresponding to the principal note of the ornament, e. g. in Nocturne op. 37 No. 1, and in Study op. 10 No. 3:

In this last case, the $G\sharp^1$ of the appoggiatura should be played simultaneously not only with the E in the bass, but also with the lower $G\sharp$ in the treble.

COMMENTARY: *Nocturnes*

1. Nocturne in B♭ minor, op. 9 No. 1

Abbreviations: FE — the original French edition (M. Schlesinger, Paris, No. 1287); GE — the original German edition (F. Kistner, Leipzig, No. 995).

Slurring, In bar 1 in the original editions the slur over the quaver-figure of the anacrusis (in bars 8 and 70 this figure has a separate slur) ends on the fourth F^2, yet in the corresponding bars 9 and 71 it ends on the third F^2 as shown in our edition. The motive of a minim + a crotchet has a separate slur in bars 2, 4, 10, 12, 13, 14, 75 and 76. In bars 15, 16, 77 and 78, which contain the same motive, most of the slurs are inadvertently omitted in both FE and GE. In bars 71−72, however, the original editions have the phrasing given here and repeated in bars 1−2. In bar 7, the original editions begin a new slur on the first crotchet in the right hand. Logic and consistency (i. e. by analogy with bars 1−2) require $D\flat^2$ to be included in the phrase here (as given in the Klindworth edition). In bar 16 the first two notes F^3-$D\flat^3$ have a separate slur. The original editions introduce a variant in bar 74; they start the slur (contrary to bar 12) on the first crotchet in the treble. FE and GE have no slur at the beginning of the bar. The slurring is inaccurate and inconsistent in the middle part in the original editions (bar 19 sqq.). In bars 20 and 28 the slurs end on the octave C^1-C^2. Bars 23, 31 etc. have no slurs at all, and in the motive in bars 25, 32, 33 etc. the slur usually ends on the last crotchet. In bars 37 and 45 one slur ends on the first octave F^1-F^2, and a new one begins on the second octave F^1-F^2. Bars 51 and 53 have no slurs. In bar 55 the slur does not begin until the first quaver in the bar, and in bars 61, 63 and 65 a new slur begins on the second half of the bar.

Bar 3. FE places a *portamento* dot also over the fifteenth note in the passage, i.e. over C^2; in GE the dots are continued until the seventeenth note inclusive. In our opinion, the legato should begin with the fifteenth note, i.e. at the beginning of the turn, which forms a single distinct group.

Bar 4. FE and GE have an accent under the minim $D\flat^2$ and not, as in bar 2, a *diminuendo* sign.

Bar 5. In the original editions, the upper voice runs as follows:

the same applies to bars 38 and 46.

Bar 17. In the original editions and in most re-

cent editions, the figure eight, indicating *all'ottava*, appears at the beginning of the bar instead of over the note $D\flat^3$. This may lead to a misunderstanding and to the consequent playing of the grace note $B\flat^1$ an octave higher, though it is clearly the same $B\flat^1$ as at the beginning of bar 16.

Bars 38 and 46. In the original editions the eighth quaver in the bass is written as A (and not $B\flat\flat$).

Bar 73. FE — probably erroneously — groups three quavers in the right hand to each of the first three quavers in the left hand, beginning the melisma of 20 notes on the fourth quaver in the left hand.

Bar 76. Contrary to the corresponding bar 14, FE and GE have F^1 and not A^1 as the last note in the bass. Some recent editions follow this version in both bars.

Bar 81. The fingering 5 4 is found in FE, GE, and also in the Oxford edition.

Bar 83. GE gives C^1 natural (not C^1 flat) as the penultimate quaver in the bar. Although probably a mistake, in view of the fact that the work ends in the major, this version might be acceptable and even advantageous.

Bars 84−85. FE and GE give one pedal for these two bars.

2. Nocturne in E♭ major, op. 9 No. 2

Abbreviations as for Nocturne op. 9 No. 1. FE gives the metronome mark as $\quad = 132$, GE as $\quad = 132$. This is an obvious error. We accept the tempo given by Mikuli.

Slurring and articulation in the right hand. By beginning the slurs in bars 1 and 2 on the first note of the bar, the original editions do not take the anacrusis into consideration. The same editions end the slur in bar 2 on the last note of the bar. In bar 3 only the notes G^2-D^2 are joined, and in bar 5 only the first two notes of the bar. In bars 6, 14 and 22 the slur ends on the dotted crotchet $B\flat^2$, in bar 8 on the last semiquaver D^2, and in bar 10 on the dotted crotchet $E\flat^2$. In bar 9 the second and third notes are slurred, and the fourth and the fifth. Bars 11 and 19 have no slurs at all. We have added a long slur in bars 7, 15 and 23, an upper slur in bars 12 and 20, a long slur from the first to the third beats of bars 13 and 21, and a shorter one on the last beat of the same bars. In bar 25 the original editions do not begin the slur until the second note in the bar. In bar 26 sqq. we follow the original slurring.

We have given the fingering from the Oxford edition as the authentic fingering of Chopin: in bars 4 and 6 (5th or 4th finger slides over two adjacent notes), bars 7 and 15 (fingers 4 1) and in bar 18 (fingers 2 1). In bars 16 and 26—28 the Oxford edition gives the same fingering as that referred to below.

We give some embellishment variants quoted in the Oxford edition as being authentically by Chopin: Nos. 1—3 according to the Oxford edition and Nos. 4—11 according to Mikuli who published this Nocturne separately because of these variants; here they are taken from Brugnoli's edition. We leave it to the performer to judge whether all these variants are of advantage to the piece as a whole. Though they are subtle, elegant and certainly the work of a master, in our opinion they may easily give rise to a certain *préciosité* and overburden the work, especially if they are not executed with the greatest precision and delicacy.

1) Bar 22 (instead of the last two semiquavers *C¹-G²* in the treble)

2) Bars 31—32

3) The ending

4) Bar 4 (over the last three quavers)

5) Bar 8

6) Bars 14—15

7) Bar 16

8) Bars 22—23

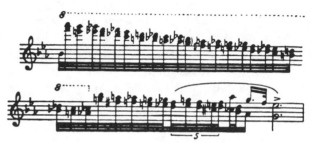

9) Bar 24

10) Bars 31—32

11) The ending

Bar *2*. FE and GE indicate a turn over the quaver *C²*. But the turn should begin on the principal note *C²*, and should be understood as a quintuplet in equal notes. Recent editions (including Mikuli) give this sign *after* the note to emphasize that the turn should begin after the principal note *C²*. This, however, may easily cause a lengthening of the principal note and too rapid an execution of the turn. In the original editions the flat and the natural are not given for the notes *D♭²* and *B¹* in the turn, though these should most certainly be played. In FE the sign of the turn is reversed. GE gives the correct sign. The same applies to bar 26.

Bars 7 and 15. The original editions do not give a natural before the Eb^2 at the end of the trill. The trill should obviously begin on the principal note.

Bar 16. The fingering of the melisma in the demisemiquavers is here given according to FE and GE, except that instead of the fingering 3 and 2, which we have at the end of the figure, the original editions give 2 and 1. The triplet sign under the last notes of the melisma is not found in FE. The same edition gives the octave D-D^1 as the fifth quaver in the bass; in the copy belonging to Chopin's sister, Madame Jędrzejewicz, the lower D is altered in pencil to an F, the version given in GE. In the second half of the bar, in both FE and GE the note Eb^1 is missing in the chord of the third and sixth quavers in the bass. We have repeated the version given in bar 8.

Bar 26. The original editions give the chord G-Bb-Eb^1 as the eighth quaver in the bass. We have given the same version as in bars 25, 28 and 29.

Bars 26−28. The fingering here is the same as in FE and GE except for the fingering 4 and 2 in bar 27 which is our addition.

Bar 30. GE does not give the mordent sign (*tr*).

Bar 34. As in FE, we tie the penultimate bass note (Bb) of the penultimate bar to the Bb in the first chord in the last bar. In GE, however, probably owing to a misreading of the slur in the manuscript, the last bass note (a Bb an octave lower) in the penultimate bar is tied to the Bb in the first chord in the last bar.

3. Nocturne in B major, op. 9 No. 3

Abbreviations as for Nocturne op. 9 No. 1.

Slurring. The slurring in the treble in the original editions is so fragmentary, incomplete, arbitrary and inconsistent that it needs to be completely changed and supplemented. It would be impossible and even unnecessary to cite here all the modifications which we have introduced, some of which follow those to be found in some recent editions. We shall draw attention only to these which may be disputable. In bar 4 FE and GE end the slur on the first note in the bar. In subsequent repetitions of this bar they give no slur (with the obvious exception where the duration of the first note is lengthened). We follow the phrasing of Mikuli, applying it by analogy in bars 24−25. In bars 13, 15, 17 and similar bars, we start the slur at the beginning of the bar, also following Mikuli's edition, though the first $C\sharp^2$ in these bars might be understood not only as the beginning of a new phrase, but also as the ending of the preceding phrase. In bar 31 FE and GE end one slur on the fifth semiquaver, and the second slur, beginning on the ninth semiquaver, finishes on the penultimate semiquaver. We have added a slur between bars 47 and 48. We have left the slur between bars 48 and 49 as in the original editions, though the notation in the corresponding bars 72−73 would by analogy require a different phrasing in bar 48. It is possible, however, that this variant was intentional. In bars 45 and 69 we begin the slur on the first note of the bar, presuming that theoretically the phrase begins here, as in bars 41 and 65. In bar 156 FE and GE end the slurs on the sixth semiquaver in both the bass and the treble.

Pedalling. Contrary to the first two numbers in this opus, in which FE and GE give exact indications of the pedalling, the original editions do not give any pedal marks in this Nocturne except under the final cadenza and at the beginning of bar 156 where, after the mark *Ped.*, there is no appropiate sign. In the copy belonging to Chopin's sister, Madame Jędrzejewicz, there is an indication (added in pencil) that the pedal should be lifted after the last bar. Mikuli has the same indication.

Bar 3. Neither FE nor GE gives a natural in front of the notes $A\sharp$ and $A\sharp^1$ in the bass. The same can be seen in all those corresponding bars where the phrase is repeated later on in the work. In bars 11 and 142 GE adds sharps in front of the seventh and eighth semiquavers in the treble, and in bar 31 gives $B\sharp^2$-$C\sharp^2$ and not B^2-C^3 as the fifth and sixth semiquavers. In both cases this corresponds to the above-mentioned $A\sharp$ in the bass, which is clearly accepted in GE. In the corresponding passages FE gives naturals in front of $C\sharp^3$ and $A\sharp^2$, which seems to indicate that the editors of this version consider that both in this bar and in all the corresponding bars there should be A in the bass and not $A\sharp$ (in spite of the absence of naturals, as already mentioned). It should be noted that in the copy belonging to Chopin's sister, Madame Jędrzejewicz, a natural was added in pencil in bars 3 and 142 in front of $A\sharp$ in the bass.

Bars 6−7. In FE and GE, the note E^2 in the treble is not tied from bar 6 to 7. We give the version of bars 26−27 and 137−138, where this note is tied. We do not, however, tie the minim E^3 (which in view of the beat should be divided rather into two tied crotchets) to the last quaver in the bar, as do FE and GE both in bar 26 and bar 137 (but not in bar 6). All recent editions, including Mikuli's, have the version which is given here.

Bar 16. The fingering 5 5 for the first two quavers in the treble is reproduced from FE and GE.

Bar 31. The fingering for the 4th, 5th, 6th, 12th and 14th semiquavers is found in FE and GE.

Bar 47. The original editions do not mark the last three semiquavers as a triplet. The whole group in the second half of the bar should be understood more as a septuplet, as can also be seen from the graphic arrangement of the notes in these editions.

B a r s *50.* The original editions give the fourth note in the bass as *A.* Following recent editions, we give the more appropriate *G♯♯*; the same applies at bar 74.

B a r s *66—67.* FE and GE do not tie the *B³* from bar 66 to bar 67. We follow the version given by Mikuli and other recent editors.

B a r s *70—71.* FE does not tie *G♯²* from bar 70 to bar 71.

B a r *79.* Although there are four demisemiquavers in the treble to each quaver in the bass, we do not think that Chopin really intended to divide them equally. This kind of passage is always treated by Chopin with great freedom. GE gives a sharp in front of *B²*, the sixth note in the treble, but does not give one in front of the following *B¹*, the eighteenth note in the treble.

B a r s *88—89.* Here and in the corresponding bars 96—97 and 120—121 we accept the authority of Mikuli's edition and tie the notes in the middle voices from one half of the bar to the other. Yet we have serious doubts as to whether this was Chopin's intention. If he really wanted to have the syncopation from one half of the bar to the other, it is remarkable that FE and GE do not give it in crotchets, as in the following bars 90, 91, 99, 122, 123. In these bars we have changed the notation for one more suitable to the given time-signature and more consistent in view of the accepted syncopation. The notation of the original editions, however, is as follows:

and

It is worth noting that the phrase is repeated three times, each time without the ties referred to above.

B a r *98.* We keep the version of the original editions with its slight variant in the rhythm in the middle voices. Recent editions give an exact repetition of the version of bar 122.

B a r *99.* The upper voice has only the value of a minim in FE and GE, with no complementary rest. Bar 123 is the same. We follow Mikuli, though the version with the minim is perhaps more appropriate and more faithful to Chopin's intentions.

B a r *113.* For the sake of complete accordance with bar 107, either *B♯¹* and not *B¹* should be in the chord in bar 113 or, in bar 107, *A¹* and not *A♯¹*. But the original version does not admit of such uniformity, and Chopin clearly never intended to introduce such a rigid conformity. Some recent editions have changed *B¹* to *B♯¹* in bar 113.

B a r *!14.* FE and GE do not give *B¹* in the chord on the third beat of the bar.

B a r *129.* FE and GE write the chord in the treble in minims.

B a r *56.* FE and Mikuli indicate *alla breve.*

4. *Nocturne in F major, op. 15 No. 1*

A b b r e v i a t i o n s : FE — the original French edition (M. Schlesinger, Paris, No. 1529); GE — the original German edition (Breitkopf & Härtel, Leipzig, No. 5502).

N o t a t i o n . In the main section of the piece we give the bass notation as in GE, which is accepted by the majority of recent editions. The notation in FE is much less clear and rational. In bar 1 it appears as follows:

The bass notation in FE is similar in bars 2—3, 9—12 and 19—24. In bar 4, however, the crotchet tails apply not only to the upper note at the beginning of each triplet, but also to all the lower notes, thus:

The same applies to bar 5, in the frist triplet in bar 6, in the first and second triplets in bar 7, in the second and third triplets in bar 8, etc. Klindworth and Brugnoli have accepted this notation in their editions, but have followed the FE notation of bar 4 etc. throughout the whole of the first section of the Nocturne, i.e. also in bars 1—3, 9—12, etc. Thus they have prolonged not only the upper but also the lower note, giving both the value of a crotchet:

In this way the characteristic movement of the accompaniment:

completely disappears and a contrary movement may easily become obtrusive:

which ought to be carefully avoided in the execution of this Nocturne.

In the middle section of the Nocturne, there is the problem of the rhythm of the melody in relation to the acompaniment. The semiquaver movement here is in ⅜ rhythm, i.e. the semiquavers are in 3 groups of 2 and not in sextuplets (2 groups of triplets). But as Chopin maintains ¾ time we must in consequence accept that in bars 29, 30 and similar bars the dotted quaver + semiquaver should be played accordingly, i.e. the semiquaver should be played between the last two semiquavers of the corresponding sextuplet in the accompaniment. The original editions, however, do not show this clearly. In bar 29, FE places the semiquaver in the bass under the fifth semiquaver in the corresponding group in the treble; similarly bars 30 and 41—44. In bars 31, 33 and 35 the same applies to the semiquaver in the upper voice which in FE is placed over the fifth semiquaver of the figure. In bars 45—47, however, FE consistently places the semiquaver in the melody over the last semiquaver in the corresponding group in the accompaniment. GE has the notation mentioned above throughout this middle section, and we have accepted this graphical arrangement. We think, however, that the semiquaver in the melody should always be played slightly before the last semiquaver of the sextuplet in the accompaniment. In our opinion this note should never be played together with the fifth semiquaver of the figure, because the melody would then lose its distinct, dotted rhythm, changing:

Bar 3. FE and GE begin a new slur on the first note in the treble, as in bar 51.

Bars 7—9. In the treble, FE begins a slur on the minim E^2, ends it on B^1 in bar 8, and then starts a new slur on the triplet in bar 8 which ends on the following minim in bar 9. GE ends the slur on the minim in bar 7, then starts a new slur on the triplet in this bar and ends it at the close of bar 8; there is a fresh slur over bar 9.

Bar 8. FE gives the value of a crotchet only to the top note of the arpeggio, $G\sharp$. The same applies to the A in the last chord in the preceding bar, and to bars 55 and 56. The change from the first to the third finger on the $G\sharp$ in bar 8 is given in the Oxford edition as Chopin's own. This fingering, marked in pencil, is also found in the FE copy belonging to Chopin's sister, Madame Jędrzejewicz.

Bar 14. The numbers 2 3 over the two C^1's in the second triplet in the bass are found in the Oxford edition and in the FE copy belonging to Chopin's sister.

Bars 19 and 21. Both here and in bars 67 and 69 the note G in the bass is given in FE as a quaver, and in GE as a crotchet.

Bar 20. In FE the note B in the bass is given as a quaver, even with a *staccato* dot, as in bar 68. In GE it has the value of a crotchet.

Bar 22. FE and GE do not break the slur at the beginning of the bar or in bar 70.

Bar 26. The Oxford edition and the FE copy belonging to Chopin's sister give the fingering 2 1 3 2 in the bass. In a similar passage in bar 28, the first six notes in the bass have the fingering: 5 3 1 3 2 1.

Bar 35. In the bass GE gives the F^1 alone instead of an octave.

Bar 41. FE and GE have only a short slur in the bass joining the semiquaver with the following crotchet, as in bar 43. In bars 42 and 44 the semiquaver is slurred with the following minim.

Bar 56. FE and GE have a slur beginning on the second E^2 in the preceding bar. Both editions give a fresh slur over bar 57.

Bar 62. In FE, the lower F is missing in the second chord of the bar.

Bars 73 and 74. In the copy belonging to Chopin's sister, Madame Jędrzejewicz, the change of pedal is transferred from the end of bar 73 to the fourth note in bar 74. This seems to indicate that Chopin meant the G^2 in the treble at the beginning of bar 74 to be held.

5. *Nocturne in F♯ major, op. 15 No. 2*

Abbreviations as for Nocturne op. 15 No. 1.

Bar 3. The fingering 1 2 1 is found in the Oxford edition and also in the FE copy belonging to Madame Jędrzejewicz, where it was added in pencil. Both in this bar and in bars 5, 9 and similar bars in the recapitulation, GE consistently gives a separate slur over the last two quavers. FE is not consistent in this matter. We retain the slurring given in FE in bars 1 and 53.

Bar 11. In the right hand the original editions slur the first five groups, each consisting of three small notes, the 22nd—24th notes, and the last six small notes as well as the whole of the second part from the sixteenth note onwards.

Bar 12. In the copy belonging to Madame Jędrzejewicz, the indication *i due Ped.* (i.e. *una corda* as well as the usual *con pedale*) is added in pencil. The same applies to bars 18 and 58.

Bars 22 and 23. The original editions slur each half bar separately.

Bars 25—32. We retain the graphical arrangement of GE. In FE, the second quaver in the bass is placed under the third semiquaver in the treble and the fourth quaver under the penultimate semiquaver in the treble.

Bar 27. In the bass the original editions give $G\sharp\sharp$ instead of A. We have changed this, the given chord being the diminished seventh of the VIIth degree in C♯ major: $B\sharp$-$D\sharp$-$F\sharp$-A.

Bars 29—46. We have added the slurs in the treble.

Bar 54. The fifth finger on the second and seventh demisemiquavers is given in the Oxford edition and is added in pencil in the copy belonging to Madame Jędrzejewicz.

Bars 60—62. The original editions give no slur in the bass.

Bar 62. In the original editions the slur does not include the $A\sharp^1$ in the treble, ending on the last note in the preceding bar. In the copy belonging to

Madame Jędrzejewicz, the following version is written in pencil:

6. Nocturne in G minor, op. 15 No. 3

Abbreviations as for Nocturne op. 15 No. 1.
Slurring. The original editions end the slur on the last note in bars 52, 56, 57, 64 and 68. We, ourselves, have added the upper slurs in bars 51—55 and 59—63. In bars 80, 82 and 84, the original editions give the slurs over the first two quavers only. In bars 89—120 we retain the slurring given for the treble in the original editions, except that in bar 105 we begin the slur at the beginning of the bar, while FE and GE begin it on the preceding G^1. In the bass they slur the first two notes in bars 89—90 and 105—106, and the six notes in bars 103—104. They also give slurs in bars 96—98, but FE ends the slur on the last crotchet in bar 97, and GE on the minim in bar 98 (and 114).

Bar 54. The original editions give $D\sharp$ instead of $E\flat$. We have noted the enharmonic change here (cf. bar 55).

Bar 76. In this bar we have the same chord, $B\sharp$-$D\sharp$-$F\sharp$-A, which has already appeared with the same notation in the preceding bar. In bar 79 it resolves appropriately onto $C\sharp$-$E\sharp$-$G\sharp$ (=V in $F\sharp$ minor). In bar 76 Chopin notates C instead of $B\sharp$, while in bars 77—78, where the chord appears three times in alternation with the chord $E\sharp$-$G\sharp$-B-D (=VII[7] in $F\sharp$ minor, but with F instead of $E\sharp$, as given by Chopin), the original editions give C instead of $B\sharp$, and $E\flat$ instead of $D\sharp$. We have notated it as $B\sharp$-$D\sharp$-$F\sharp$-A throughout. In the chord at the beginning of bar 76 GE gives a sharp in front of C^1, thus changing C^1 ($B\sharp$ according to our notation) to $C\sharp^1$. This version was also accepted by Mikuli, but in our opinion, the version with C ($B\sharp$!) given by Klindworth is correct. In bars 75 and 76 FE does not give sharps in front of the octave $C\sharp$ in the bass on the second beat of the bar, which is obviously an omission.

Bar 151. In FE, both the bottom D's are tied. FE and GE give *pp* here, we have transferred this indication to bar 149 by analogy with the corresponding bar 133.

7. Nocturne in $C\sharp$ minor, op. 27 No. 1

Abbreviations: FE — the original French edition (M. Schlesinger, Paris, No. 1935); GE — the original German edition (Breitkopf & Härtel, Leipzig, No. 5666).

Slurring. The original editions begin fresh slurs in bars 6, 22, 89, 90 and 98, do not break the slur at the beginning of bar 7, and finish the slur at the end of bars 15, 22, 65, 68 (the slur begun in bar 67), 73 (the slur begun in bar 71), 89, 92, 93, 95 and 97. No slur is given in bar 45.

Bars 7 and 23. Unlike the original editions, we have given the E^1 in the bass to the right hand.

Bars 13—14. The indication, which is repeated several times, for the use of the fifth finger in the bass is found in the Oxford edition and is also added in pencil in the copy of FE belonging to Chopin's sister, Madame Jędrzejewicz.

Bars 27—28. According to the Oxford edition, Chopin took the fourth, ninth and tenth quavers in bar 27, and the third, fourth and ninth in bar 28 with the right hand.

Bars 41 and 43. In bar 41, the original editions give B^1 and not $G\sharp^1$ as the penultimate quaver, contrary to bar 43, where in the corresponding place it gives $G\sharp^1$ and not B^1. We have accepted the version given by Mikuli and followed by other recent editors as being more logical and rational, continuing the steady progression in tenths between the lowest and the highest notes of the bass figure in each bar.

Bars 67, 71 and 75. GE gives a *tr* instead of a mordent. FE gives no indication in bars 67 and 71, and in bar 75 marks a mordent. In bar 67 FE does not give the indication *stretto*.

Bars 78—81. Here, just two chords of the diminished seventh are alternated, i.e. the chord VII[7] in C major (B-D-F-$A\flat$) and VII[7] in G major ($F\sharp$-A-C-$E\flat$), i.e. the dominant and dominant of the dominant in C major. In bar 81 the chord VII[7] in G major, enharmonically changed, becomes VII[7] in $C\sharp$ minor. Chopin changes the notation of the chords in bars 78—80, probably so as to lead to the upper voices in sixths.

Bar 83. FE gives a pause above the upper staff over just the first octave in the recitative. So does GE, but additionally it gives a bar-line in the upper staff over this octave. The pause seems to imply holding the last chord before the recitative, which is why we have placed it over this chord and in the bass. In any case, the pause cannot mean that the first octave in the recitative should be held.

Bar 84. At the beginning of this bar in the bass recent editions have $_1C\sharp$ as a grace note, or an arpeggio octave $_1C\sharp$-$C\sharp$. We have followed FE, GE and Mikuli's version. The use of this octave is, however, very advisable.

8. Nocturne in $D\flat$ major, op. 27 No 2.

Abbreviations as for Nocturne op. 27 No. 1.
Bar 7. FE ties the $E\flat^2$'s in the treble, but does not give a turn sign. GE gives a turn, but does not tie the $E\flat^2$'s. We follow Mikuli's version.

Bar 8. The last four numbers indicating the fingering (1 4 2 1) are given according to the Oxford edition, which is supported by the FE copy belonging to Chopin's sister, Madame Jędrzejewicz.

Bar 10. Neither in FE nor in GE is the note F^2, at the beginning of the bar in the treble, tied to the F^2 of the preceding bar. The appropriate slur is missing, probably by mistake (cf. bars 33—34 and 53—54).

Bar 13. The fingering of the triplet in the treble and the preceding Cb^3 (4 $\frac{2}{1}$) is taken from the Oxford edition as Chopin's own indication. Starting from the sixth Db^2-Bb^2, the original editions give both voices separately, which is an unnecessary complication, and makes the reading more difficult. We have accepted Klindworth's notation.

Bar 14. GE gives Gb^2-Bb^2 and not Eb^2-Gb^2 as the fifth third in the sextuplet in the treble.

Bar 17. FE gives Bbb and not Eb as the last semiquaver in the bass, as in the seventh semiquaver.

Bars 19 and 21. The fourth finger on Db in the bass is indicated in FE and in GE.

Bar 21. In the second half of the bar, Brugnoli repeats the following variant given by J. Fontana:

Bars 22—25. Although he only partially emphasized this in his notation, it is obvious that Chopin intended the following progression:

Bar 23. GE gives the D, a third higher, not B as the seventh semiquaver in the bass.

Bar 25. In GE the bass moves as follows:

Bars 25—26. In bar 25 FE and GE indicate a *crescendo* under the semiquaver group, and in bar 26 they do not indicate *pp*. The Oxford edition gives no *crescendo* and has the sign *pp*. In the copy of Madame Jędrzejewicz the *crescendo* is crossed out, and the indication *pp* is added in bar 26.

Bar 27. FE and GE do not tie the two Ab^1's. We follow Mikuli's version, which is the same as in bars 3 and 47.

Bars 29—30. The original editions do not bring out the progression Db^1-D^1-Eb^1 in the bass with

sufficient clarity. We have added quaver tails to these notes, following the edition of Sauer (Edition Schott).

Bar 33. GE gives Ab^1, not F^1, as the second and fourth semiquavers in the bass.

Bar 34. In GE the penultimate sixth in the treble has the value of a demisemiquaver, after which comes a rest of the same value, while the last sixth has the value of a semiquaver. FE has basically the same version, but prints the last sixth (of quaver value) after the last semiquaver in the bass, as if it had a demisemiquaver value. We follow Mikuli's version, though the version in GE may represent a rhythmic variant intended by Chopin.

Bar 40. FE and GE begin the slur on the second quaver in the treble.

Bars 42—44. FE and GE give lengthened accent signs after the *sf* signs. In bar 43 this accent in fact looks like a *diminuendo*. We have placed the accents over the appropriate notes, as in the Scholtz edition.

Bars 44—45. The fingering in the bass in bar 44 and in the treble in bar 45 (starting from the fifth semiquaver) is taken from the Oxford edition as Chopin's own.

Bar 45. FE and GE give a long *diminuendo* sign after *f*, and the word *diminuendo*. The Oxford edition, however, adds *crescendo* after *f* in bar 45 and *fff* in bar 46. In the copy belonging to Madame Jędrzejewicz, this *crescendo* and *fff* are also written in pencil in place of the word *diminuendo*, which is crossed out.

Bar 50. The indication *pp* is found in the Oxford edition, and is added in pencil in the copy belonging to Madame Jędrzejewicz.

Bar 52. FE and GE indicate *con forza* at the beginning of the bar. These words are crossed out in pencil in the copy belonging to Madame Jędrzejewicz, and instead the word *riten.* appears to have been written. The fingering 5 3 2 1 4 in the second half of the bar and the reoccurrence of the third finger several times in the first half of the bar are taken from the Oxford edition. Though the notes in the right hand may be evenly distributed against the notes in the bass, we do not think that in the less regularly constructed second half of this passage Chopin wished them to be in groups of four.

Bar 59. GE gives F and not Db as the third semiquaver in the bass.

Bar 60. The fingering of the right-hand passage is taken from the Oxford edition.

Bars 66—71. GE marks *Ped.* at the beginning of bar 66, and lifts it only at the end of bar 71.

Bar 78. FE ties the Ab of the penultimate bar to the Ab in the final chord. Instead of this, GE slurs the lowest notes in the last two chords.

9. Nocturne in B major, op. 32 No. 1

Abbreviations: FE — the original French edition (M. Schlesinger, Paris, No. 2500); GE — the original German edition (A. M. Schlesinger, Berlin, No. 2180).

Bar 4. GE does not give a mordent over the third semiquaver in the bar. The original editions end the slur on the last note of the bar.

Bar 7. The fingering in the bass is taken from the Oxford edition. In bar 19 the same edition gives the third finger on $F\sharp$, while in the copy belonging to Madame Jędrzejewicz the fourth finger is marked in pencil.

Bar 8. FE and GE give D^1-F^1 as the third quaver in the bass, and not D^1-$E\sharp^1$, which is more appropriate. Chopin himself notates $E\sharp^1$ and not F^1 in the corresponding passage in bar 10.

Bars 8—9. The *crescendo* and *decrescendo* signs are found in the Oxford edition and in the copy belonging to Madame Jędrzejewicz. The same applies to the *decrescendo* sign in bar 12.

Bars 8—10. As in FE, both here and in bars 33 and 54 we have added a crotchet tail to the last quaver in the bass in order to emphasize that the note should also be held at the beginning of the following bar. (This is a simplified but comprehensible notation and has also been followed in other recent editions.) We have added similar tails in bars 31, 32, 52 and 53. In these bars GE does not give any crotchet tails whatsoever in the bass.

Bar 12. As in the Oxford edition and following the indication in the copy of Madame Jędrzejewicz, the first finger is given twice in succession in the bass.

Bars 13—14. Here the question arises whether the different version in the bass, as compared with bars 1—2, was intended by Chopin. There may be doubts as to this. Possibly it is just a mistake. It is also possible that bars 13—14 were only marked in the autograph as a repetition of bars 1—2 and were copied inaccurately. It is worth noting, in any case, that in bar 15 the bass returns to the version of bar 3, though it would be more consistent to continue the modified version of the preceding bars.

Bars 14—15. Contrary to bars 2—3, FE and GE end the slurs both in the treble and in the bass on the last note of bar 14.

Bar 16. In the first half of this bar GE repeats the first four bass notes of the preceding bar (B-$F\sharp^1$-$F\sharp$-$F\sharp^1$).

Bar 21. The version in the treble is doubtful. Here and in bar 42 FE gives $C\sharp^2$ as a crotchet, not as a minim, in the first half of the bar, while GE gives $C\sharp^2$ twice in the rhythm ♩. ♪, and in these very two bars. We follow Mikuli's version suggesting, however, that the version in GE may be used as a variant in bar 42.

Bars 25—26. The fingering in the bass is taken from the Oxford edition.

Bars 27—28. The accent signs and the sign f in bar 27, and p in bar 28, together with the fingering given in our edition, are found in the Oxford edition and in the copy belonging to Madame Jędrzejewicz. FE and GE do not give these details.

Bar 28. The first note in the treble (as in bar 49) is given in FE as an appoggiatura after a quaver rest. We follow the version in GE.

Bar 29. The Oxford edition gives ff, which does not appear in FE, GE or the copy belonging to Madame Jędrzejewicz. The fingering is taken from the Oxford edition. In the copy of Madame Jędrzejewicz the fourth finger is given on B^1.

Bar 30. The fingering in the bass is taken from the Oxford edition.

Bars 37—39. The fingering in the bass is taken from the Oxford edition and the copy belonging to Madame Jędrzejewicz. The fingering given in the treble in bar 37 is to be found only in the Oxford edition.

Bar 39. In FE the group of quavers in the bass is marked as a quintuplet both here and in bar 60. We follow the GE version. Chopin himself put the second $G\sharp^1$ crotchet in the upper staff, probably in order to give it to the right hand.

Bar 40. In FE and GE the $F\sharp$ minim in the bass has no dot; bar 61 is the same.

Bar 45. GE gives the following version:

Bar 60. The fingering for the right-hand passage is taken from FE and GE.

Bar 62. In GE the chord in the treble is written with an arpeggio sign instead of the small crotchet notes given in FE. In both FE and GE the chord on which a longer section began with bar 62 is notated with an F; we have changed this F to $E\sharp$ (following Klindworth), for the chord in question is a chord of the subdominant seventh with an augmented root, $E\sharp$-G-B-D, in B minor.

Bar 63. In GE the last six chords in this section (before the final *Adagio*) are written in small notes.

Bars 64 and 65. The *Adagio* is as follows in GE:

In FE the octave B-B in the last two bars is printed in notes of normal size, while $A\sharp$-$A\sharp$ at the beginning of the penultimate bar and both the last two chords are in smaller notes. We accept the notation of recent editions as being the clearest and most reliable. The major ending in GE is worth noting; in our opinion it is very probable that the sharp in front of the *D* in the last bar was added by mistake instead of the natural, because GE notates the arpeggio in the second half of bar 63 in the same way: in front of both *D*'s there are sharps instead of naturals.

10. Nocturne in A♭ major, op. 32 No. 2

Abbreviations as for Nocturne op. 32 No. 1.

Bar *1*. FE and GE give no C^1 in the first chord, thus differing from bar 75. In FE and GE this chord, as in bar 2, has a separate arpeggio sign in each staff. In bar 75 FE does not give arpeggio sign in front of the first chord, while bar 76 has the same sign as in bar 2. GE, on the other hand, puts a long wavy line in bars 75—76 in front of both chords, unlike its version in bars 1—2. The most appropriate, in our opinion, would be a simultaneous arpeggio in both hands in bar 1 and bar 75, and a long, simple arpeggio in bar 2 and bar 76.

Bar *4*. In FE and GE the second, third and fourth notes in the treble have a separate slur here and in all further repetitions of this bar.

Bar *5*. GE does not give a turn sign either here or in bar 53.

Bar *6*. In the original editions the semiquavers in this bar are not marked as septuplets. We think that they should be grouped $2+2+3$.

Bar *9*. The original editions begin a new slur on G^2 both here and in later repetitions of this bar.

Bars *14—15*. In the original editions, the penultimate note ($D♭^1$) in the bass in bar 14 has no crotchet tail, nor has the second note in bar 15 a quaver tail. We have kept the slurring in the bass given by Mikuli and other recent editors, following FE. It is possible, however, that FE gave this slur inaccurately, and it should reach the second quaver in the bass in bar 15.

Bar *19*. FE does not give $B♭$ as the last note in the bass (unlike the corresponding bar 11), but *F*. Bars 59 and 67 are the same. We follow the GE version.

Bars *27—34*. The slurring in this passage and in the corresponding bars 39—46 shows rather considerable differences, not only between FE and GE but also between the corresponding sections in each of these editions. We have made the slurring uniform, choosing the most appropriate and most characteristic slurs. In bars 29—30 (and 41—42) in particular, we have kept the slurring which is apparently intended to vary the phrasing of the motive which is repeated four times in a row $B♭^1$-C^2-$D♭^2$-C^2-$B♭^1$-$A♭^1$.

Bar *28*. FE gives $F\sharp^1$ alone as the second quaver in the treble.

Bar *29*. GE does not give the mordent over either the fourth or the tenth quaver in the treble. To emphasize the progression in the bass, we have added a quaver stem to the sixth quaver, as in bar 33, where FE and GE add a dot to the preceding note, obviously inadvertently. The same applies to bars 41 and 45.

Bars *30* and *33*. Here also GE gives no mordent.

Bars *35—38* and *47—50*. FE has the following version:

etc.

GE has either the quavers only, or the following version:

etc.

but in bars 48—50 it has the same notation as FE. We accept the most appropriate notation, given by Klindworth, Pugno and other editors.

Bar *38*. Chopin writes the first octave in the treble as F^1-F^2. We accept the notation given by Klindworth (cf. bar 50).

Bar *40*. FE and GE, probably inadvertently, do not give a mordent at the beginning of the bar. We accept the mordent by analogy with bar 28. FE notates B-$C\sharp^1$ only (without $G\sharp$) as the second and third quavers in the bass.

Bar *47*. FE has the fifth A-E^1 as the second and third quavers in the bass. Following GE we accept the third A-$C\sharp^1$ by analogy with $A♭$-C^1 in bar 35.

Bar *50*. In FE and GE the seventh quaver in the bass is notated as $A♭$ and not as $G\sharp$ (probably to emphasize the return of the flat key).

Bar *74*. FE and GE start a new slur on the first note of this bar.

11. Nocturne in G minor, op. 37 No. 1

Abbreviations FE — the original French edition (Troupenas et Cie, Paris, No. 893); GE — the original German edition (Breitkopf & Härtel, Leipzig, No. 6334).

FE gives *Lento*, GE — *Andante sostenuto*.

Bar *6*. FE and GE indicate the third finger four times in succession. In the copy belonging to Madame Dubois, Chopin's pupil, the third finger is marked in pencil twice in succession at the beginning of bar 9 and this fingering is given in the Oxford edition.

Bar *8*. FE and GE do not give $E♭^1$ in the last chord in the bar.

Bars *10—11*. In FE, F^1 is not tied at bars 10 and 11, or at bars 26 and 27.

B a r *15*. In GE, all the small notes here and in bar 81 are written as crotchets. FE writes the embellishment C^2-D^2-C^2 in quavers, and the appoggiatura F^2 as a quaver, but unbarred.

B a r *16*. The notation of the treble is wrong and uncertain both in this bar and in its repetitions (bars 32 and 82). For these three bars we follow the version of bars 16 and 32 given in FE. In bar 82, FE notates D^1 as a minim with only one dot, after a crotchet rest.

B a r *19*. Here and in bar 31 GE gives D-G-Bb-D^1 and not G-Bb-D^1 as the second crotchet in the bass.

B a r *31*. GE gives Eb-G-C^1-G^1 as the last crotchet in the bass.

B a r *35*. In GE there is no C^1 in the last chord.

B a r *37*. After the first note in the treble FE gives only $C\sharp^1$-D^1-F^1 in small notes, withouth the following Bb^1. The same applies to bar 87.

B a r *38*. FE has the following rhythm in the treble: a crotchet (with an arpeggio), a dotted quaver, a semiquaver, a minim.

B a r *40*. In GE, instead of a crotchet rest at the beginning of the bar, the C^1 in the middle voice of the preceding bar is tied over.

B a r s *51—52*. In both these bars GE gives naturals in front of Ab in the first and fourth chords, and in bar 53 there is no Ab in the first chord in the bar, i.e. in the treble there is only C^1-Eb^1.

B a r *57*. GE adds the lower octave $_1Eb$ to the first note in the bass.

B a r *85*. GE gives two equal quavers on the second beat of the bar and not a dotted quaver + semiquaver. In FE, the turn in small notes after C^2 is not given, contrary to bar 19.

B a r *90*. GE does not give *riten.* The fingering here and in the last bar is taken from the Oxford edition.

12. Nocturne in G major, op. 37 No. 2

A b b r e v i a t i o n s as for Nocturne op. 37 No. 1.

The pedalling, which is not given in FE, is taken from GE.

S l u r r i n g. The original editions do not break the slurs at the beginning of bars 3, 6, 12, 17, 19, 70 and 73 (although in bars 17 and 19 GE begins a new slur). We have taken GE as a basis for the slurring in bars 28—67 and 83—122. FE begins new slurs at the beginning of bars 31, 37, 43, 49, 55, 61, 67, 88, 94, 101, 107, 113 and 118. The very frequent *crescendo* and *diminuendo* signs are given according to GE. FE omits nearly all of them.

B a r *1*. GE gives *Andantino*.

B a r *13*. GE ties both thirds Db^2-F^2 and prolongs Db^2 in the second third to the value of a crotchet (cf. bar 15).

B a r *22*. In FE, there is no mordent on the note D^1.

B a r *27*. In GE, there is a sharp in front of D^1, as in Mikuli.

B a r *28*. After this bar the original editions have the following bar:

According to the Oxford edition, Chopin crossed out this bar in the copy belonging to his pupil. A strict analogy with the transition to bar 83 and the following bars was thus retained. The bar mentioned above is in Mikuli's edition, but not in Klindworth's.

B a r *32*. In the original editions, instead of the tied notes in the chord, there are minims followed by a crotchet rest (and not two quaver rests). We have adopted the notation of recent editions as being more appropriate to the given metre. The same applies to all similar passages later in this section.

B a r *34*. In the original editions the second third C^1-E^1 bas the value of a dotted crotchet. Following Mikuli, we have shortened its value for technical reasons and given a quaver rest at the end of the bar, as in bars 30, 38 and similar bars in the original editions. The same applies to bars 58, 89 and 113.

B a r *43*. Both here and in the corresponding bars 67, 98 and 122 we keep the original notation for the second chord. Recent editions emphasize the middle note, i.e. the dotted crotchet. The arpeggio in this chord is not brought out sufficiently clearly. The notation is uncertain. In bars 43 and 67, it means not so much an arpeggio as the breaking of the chord. In bar 122 the arpeggio sign before the chord renders the tied grace note superfluous. In bar 98, FE gives a grace note before the arpeggio sign (GE ties it here, too). It is most probable that in all four cases the arpeggio should be preceded by the grace note. The notation is inaccurate, probably owing to a misunderstanding of the signs in the manuscript.

B a r *44*. In the original editions the lower $E\sharp$ has the value of a dotted crotchet. Following Klindworth we have shortened this note to a crotchet; we do the same in bars 45, 48, 49, 99, 100, 103 and 121. In bar 104 the original editions give a crotchet rest instead of dotting the corresponding C^1, which gives us even more justification for making this change.

B a r *52*. GE gives only *p* and not *pp*.

B a r *72*. GE and FE give the third D^2-F^2 and not $G\sharp^1$-F^2 as the last semiquaver in the treble. We follow the version given in bars 4, 5 and 71.

B a r s *83* and *84*. In GE, C^1 is not sharpened. In bar 84 GE does not indicate *sostenuto*.

B a r *90*. GE gives one long arpeggio sign for the whole chord, beginning from the lowest $C\sharp$ in the bass, and does not tie $G\sharp$ over to bar 91.

Bar *95.* In the original editions *B♯* lasts throughout the whole bar as a dotted minim.

Bar *114.* GE, obviously inadvertently, does not give the third *D¹-F♯¹* in the right-hand chord at the beginning of the bar.

Bar *115.* In GE, there is no arpeggio sign before the chord and the small note is tied to the following *C♯¹*. There is no *cresc.*, either here or in bar 119.

Bars *117-118.* In GE, the *F♯* in the bass has the value of a minim only and is followed by a crotchet rest. In FE, the last quaver, i.e. the octave *A♯¹-A♯²*, is written in the upper staff (as in GE), and a quaver rest (which is not found in GE) is added in the lower staff, which seems to indicate that the octave in question should be played with the right hand.

Bar *118.* In GE, at the beginning of the bar, *A♯¹-B¹-D♯²* is notated in small semiquaver notes, and the arpeggio sign covers all six notes in the chord.

Bar *122.* FE and GE tie the grace note *E¹* with the following *E¹* in the chord (cf. notes on bars 43 sqq.).

Bar *123.* In FE, there is no *forte* sign.

Bar *138.* GE notates *pp* here.

13. Nocturne in C minor, op. 48 No. 1

Abbreviations: FE — the original French edition (M. Schlesinger, Paris, No. 3487); GE — the original German edition (Breitkopf & Härtel, Leipzig, No. 6653); MS — the manuscript, the attested copy which served as the basis for GE, as may be seen from the similarity of the texts. This is now preserved in the Frédéric Chopin Society, Warsaw.

Fingering. In bars 1–2 the Oxford edition (Oxford University Press) indicates the third finger on the first three notes in the treble, as given by Chopin. In bar 4, the fingers 4 2 are indicated in the Oxford edition and in the FE copy which belonged to Chopin's sister, Madame Jędrzejewicz. In bar 5 FE indicates the second finger for the second crotchet in the right hand, but in the copy of Madame Jędrzejewicz this figure is crossed out in pencil. In bar 7 FE gives the third finger for *F♯¹*. In bar 8 the fourth and second fingers are marked over *B♭¹* and *G¹* both in the Oxford edition and in the copy belonging to Madame Jędrzejewicz. The same occurs in bar 9, where the first finger is given for *A♭¹*. The fifth and fourth fingers on the twelfth and thirteenth semiquavers in bar 22 are repeated from the Oxford edition and the copy belonging to Madame Jędrzejewicz. In bar 75 the figure 1 over the last semiquaver is taken from the Oxford edition.

Bar *4.* The MS gives *stretto*.

Bar *10.* In MS and GE, a crotchet tail is added to the first note of the arpeggio (*F¹-A♭¹-D♭²-F²*). In MS a similar tail is also added to the first note of the preceding arpeggio (*G♭¹*). MS and GE begin a new slur on this note. GE gives *C-A♭-E♭¹* as the second crotchet in the bass, probably by mistake.

Bar *11.* GE gives *G-C¹-E♭¹-G¹* as the last chord in the bass.

Bar *16.* MS and GE give the repetition of the preceding octave *₁B-B* and not *₁G-G* as the last octave in the bars; this is slurred with the following octave *C-C*, like the preceding *₁B♭-B* and *₁B-B*.

Bar *20.* GE gives *E♭-A♭-C¹-E♭¹* as the last chord in the bass.

Bars *24-25.* In FE, neither *C* in the treble nor the upper *C* in the bass is tied at bars 24-25.

Bar *26.* In the third chord in this bar FE does not give *G* in the bass.

Bar *27.* FE gives *A-C-E* as the second chord in the bass.

Bars *30-32.* The arpeggio sign before the first chord in bars 30 and 31 and before the last chord in bar 32 is divided between the two staves in FE. In GE the sign at the beginning of bar 30 runs through both staves, while in bars 31 and 32 it is divided. We repeat the signs according to MS.

Bars *33-37.* In these bars, MS and GE give only one slur in the treble, ending at the beginning of bar 38.

Bar *35.* MS and GE give an arpeggio sign at the beginning of the bar in the treble. We follow the FE version, analogous to that of bar 29.

Bar *43.* MS and GE do not give naturals in the second chord before the two *D♯*'s. We follow the FE version, corresponding to that of bar 35, where *D♯* appears only in the last chord. In the second chord in bar 43, MS and GE do not give *F¹*. In GE, *B-D-B* and not *G-D-B* is given as the first chord in the bass, and the last chord is written quite erroneously as *C-D♯-F-D♯¹*.

Bar *48.* Erroneously, GE gives the octave *F²-F³* and not *E²-E³* as the fifth semiquaver in the right hand. FE places a single slur over the last four triplets, while GE gives each of them a separate slur. We accept the slurring given by Mikuli.

Bar *51.* In MS and in GE, the second half of this bar is as follows:

We follow the FE version, corresponding to the version in bar 3.

Bar *52.* In MS and the original editions, the first *G¹* in the treble is not tied to the second. We have adopted the version of the recent editions, corresponding to bar 4.

Bar *55.* MS and the original editions do not tie the quaver *D¹* to the following semiquaver. We follow the version given by recent editions, corresponding to bar 7.

Bar *56.* In GE, there is no natural in front of the *B♯* in the third triplet.

B a r *58*. In GE, the second $A\flat^2$ (tied to the first one in the bar) is written as a crotchet.

B a r *60*. In GE, the second $E\flat^2$ is written as a quaver.

B a r *62*. MS and GE give an additional $E\flat^2$ to the third quaver (G^1-C^2) from the end of the bar, as in the two following quavers.

B a r *63*. MS and GE give *pp*, which is not in FE.

B a r *64*. In GE, F^1-$A\flat^1$-$B\flat^1$ is repeated as the fifth and the sixth quavers in the treble. In MS and GE there is no appoggiatura $B\flat^1$.

B a r *67*. In MS, FE and GE only the sixth C-$A\flat$ is given as the second quaver in the bass.

B a r *69*. GE has only the octave G-G^1 as the fifth quaver in the bass and there is no C^1 in the eighth and ninth quavers. This was probably due to the unclear notation in MS. The note C^2 in the original version is not tied to the following semiquaver. We follow the version given by recent editions, corresponding to bar 21.

B a r *70*. In MS and GE, there is no $B\flat$ in the second, third, fourth and fifth quavers in the bass, or D^1 in the tenth quaver in the bass.

B a r *72*. In MS and GE, the bass in the first half of the bar moves as follows·

B a r *73*. GE gives G-B and not F-B as the tenth quaver in the bass.

B a r *74*. We repeat the slurring in the bass given by GE. MS and FE continue the slurring from the preceding bar.

B a r *75*. GE adds an upper octave to the C in the bass.

14. Nocturne in F♯ minor, op. 48 No. 2

A b b r e v i a t i o n s as for Nocturne op. 48 No 1.

S l u r r i n g. MS, FE and GE do not break the slur in the treble in bar 5. The phrase might well be ended on the first quaver in the bar (as in Klindworth's edition). The beginning of the turn on $F\sharp^1$ (after the second quaver) in the corresponding bar in the recapitulation (bar 103) seems to indicate that a new phrase begins with the turn, i. e. that the preceding one ends on the second quaver in the bar. (Moreover, all the phrases in this section begin on the second crotchet in the bar, as may be seen from a closer observation.) MS and the original editions do not break the slur in bars 7, 9, 11, 13 (see above, notes on bar 5 and cf. the corresponding bar 41), 15, 17 and similar bars either. This means that in the original version one long slur, indicating *legato*, is placed over almost the entire main section of the Nocturne and its recapitulation. Again, in bars 119 and 127 the slur is not broken in the original version. In the middle section, the original ver-

sion ends the slur on the last note in bars 60 and 64 (but in the corresponding bar 80 it ends, as given in our edition, on the second crotchet), and the passage from bar 65 up to the middle of bar 69 is given only one slur in FE and GE, while MS has no slur here. In bars 132, 133 and 134, MS, FE and GE give upper slurs (as well as lower slurs) in the treble beginning on the first note in the bar and ending on the last note (before the quaver rest). We have transferred these slurs, as did Klindworth in his edition.

B a r *24*. MS and FE give the two bass figures in reverse. But in bar 52 they give the same bass notation as in our edition in bar 24.

B a r *44*. The octave $D\sharp^2$-$D\sharp^3$ with the grace note $D\sharp^2$ is given in MS and in FE as we have it here. GE ties the two lower $D\sharp^2$'s, which makes it an arpeggio octave. However, Chopin certainly intended to give both the grace note and the arpeggio octave here:

B a r *56*. The second minim in the treble should be notated as $D\sharp\sharp^1$. Chopin changes it enharmonically to E^1 in view of the following $D\flat$ major (which, to facilitate reading, replaces the appropriate $C\sharp$ major).

B a r *57*. MS, FE and GE give *molto più lento*, but in the copy belonging to Chopin's sister, Madame Jędrzejewicz, the word *molto* in crossed out; the Oxford edition omits it, too.

B a r *63*. MS and GE give the indication *p*.

B a r *66*. The arpeggio sign before the chord with the appoggiatura is here in the form given by FE and GE, i.e. as a slur and not as a wavy line. It indicates the following execution:

The same applies to bars 68, 82 and 84.

B a r *69*. Both here and in bar 85 we have repeated the notation given in FE. The notation in GE is as given at *a* and in MS as given at *b*:

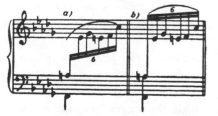

MS and GE have no arpeggio signs before the preceding chord, and in the corresponding bar 85 GE even ties the $B\flat$'s in the first two chords.

B a r *70*. MS, FE and GE do not give C^2 in the first chord in the bar. We have repeated the version of bar 86. The same applies to G^1 at the beginning of bar 71.

Bar 72. FE does not indicate *ritenuto*.

Bar 75. The Oxford edition gives *pp*, Mikuli in his edition gives *f*.

Bars 82–83. In MS and FE, $_1A\flat$ is not tied at bars 82 and 83.

Bar 92. MS, FE and GE do not give the grace note $D\sharp^1$. Following Mikuli we have repeated this from bar 76.

Bar 95. In GE, the two $B\flat$'s in the first two chords in the bar are tied.

Bar 96. MS and GE give the following rhythm:

Bar 98. In FE and in GE, the note $D\flat^2$ at the beginning of the bar has the value of a quaver. GE does not give the crotchet $A\flat^1$ on the second beat of the bar. MS has the figure 9 over the last semi-quavers of the run, which leads to the conclusion that four semiquavers should be played on the second beat of the bar and the rest on the third beat. In GE, the figure 9 is placed, apparently in error, over the upper part of the passage, while FE does not give it at all.

Bar 104. In MS and in GE, the last five notes in the treble are joined and marked as a quintuplet.

Bars 105–106. In the second half of bar 105 and in the first of bar 106, Chopin notates $F\sharp\sharp$ instead of G in the bass, giving the latter only in the second half of bar 106 in the left hand.

Bar 109. At the end of the trill, MS, FE and GE give clearly $D\sharp^2$ and not $D\sharp\sharp^2$, which is found in Mikuli's edition and has been accepted by most recent editions. $D\sharp\sharp^2$ would be more appropriate if there were a major and not a minor triad in the second half of the bar.

Bar 127. Unlike bar 129, MS, FE and GE do not give the crotchet $F\sharp^2$ on the second beat of the bar here (as well as the dotted minim), as required by the part-movement.

Bar 131. At the beginning of the bar, the upper crotchet $F\sharp$ is not given in GE.

Bar 137. At the beginning of the bar, MS and FE give the octave $F\sharp$-$F\sharp$ in the bass. In the preceding bar GE and Mikuli do not begin the scale until after the last note in the bass. This delaying of the scale gives too tranquil an effect, especially with the usual *ritenuto*. This is why we have adopted the version of MS and FE.

15. Nocturne in F minor, op. 55 No. 1

Abbreviations: FE — the original French edition (M. Schlesinger, Paris, No. 4084); GE — the original German edition (Breitkopf & Härtel, Leipzig, No. 7142).

Slurring. In bars 1–7 we keep the slurring given in GE which, though subsequently inconsistent, shows best that the phrase begins with the anacrusis C^2 (and not just with F^2) both at the beginning of the piece (bars 1–2) and in the two following repeats. FE begins new slurs on the note F^2 in bars 3 and 5 and on the minim in bar 7. In bars 16–24 the original editions give a very arbitrary and incorrect slurring. It should be noted that FE begins new slurs in bars 17 and 19 on the first quaver in the bar. In bar 24 we have begun a new slur on the third crotchet, since we consider that the phrase ends on the second crotchet, as in bars 16, 18, 20, 21, 22 and 23 (cf. also bar 8). The original editions give one legato slur over bars 77–96.

Fingering. We take the fingering from the Oxford edition in bars 60 (in the bass), 64 (in the bass), 69–70 (5 1 4 1 5 3 in the treble), 71–72 (the lowest voice in the bass), 77–80 (until the first quaver in bar 80 inclusive, with the exception of the second 4 5 in bar 78), 85 (the first finger on $G\flat$ and F in the bass). In bar 86 the Oxford edition indicates the fingers 4 2 on the fifth and sixth quavers, and on the eighth, ninth and tenth, 1 4 2. The fingering 1 4 2 is also given on the fourth, fifth, sixth, eighth, ninth and tenth quavers in bar 88, and then 3 1. In bar 89 the first finger is given on the first quaver, and 2 4 on the last two quavers. In bar 91, fingers 2 4 are given on the fifth and sixth quavers.

Bar 6. In the original editions there is no $E\flat^1$ in the chord on the second beat of the bar either here or in bar 14, but this note is given in the corresponding bar 46.

Bar 14. In FE, the embellishment at the end of the bar is written in demisemiquavers without any *staccato* dots.

Bar 15. Both here and in bars 31 and 47 GE ties the grace note $B\flat$ to the next chord. This must have arisen from a misunderstanding of the arpeggio sign in the manuscript.

Bar 19. In the original editions there is no D in the last chord in the bass. We have added one to correspond with bar 35.

Bars 19 and 35. Both here and in bars 17 and 33 GE has equal quavers on the second beat of the bar. We follow the version given by Mikuli and FE.

Bar 30. In FE, there is also C^1 between $A\flat$ and $E\flat^1$ in the chord on the second beat of the bar.

Bar 48. At the beginning of the bar GE gives the fifth in the bass an octave higher.

Bar 56. FE and GE give G-D-$B\flat$ as the last chord in the bass. GE has no arpeggio sign.

Bar 59. GE gives $D\flat$ and not C as the third note of the second triplet in the bass. At the beginning of the bar it does not give the arpeggio sign before the sixth F^1-$G\flat^2$ (nor does it give it at the beginning of bars 61 and 63).

Bar 62. In GE the note $E\flat^2$ at the beginning of the bar is tied to the preceding bar.

Bars *72–73*. In FE and in GE (as in the editions of Mikuli and Klindworth), the note C^2 is not tied at bars 72–73. Some editions (Pugno, Brugnoli, Cortot) tie this C^2 by analogy with bars 1, 8–9, 10–11, 12–13 etc.

Bars *73–74*. According to the Oxford edition, Chopin played the lowest notes in the bass F-G-$A\flat$-E with their lower octaves.

Bar *82*. FE gives only the fifth $B\flat$-F^1 as the second crotchet in the bass.

Bar *83*. At the beginning of the bar GE gives only the lower $D\flat$ in the bass without its upper octave.

Bar *84*. The original editions have $C\flat$-$A\flat$ and not B-$A\flat$ on the second beat of the bar.

Bar *94*. GE repeats the chord in the bass.

Bars *99* and *101*. FE and GE divide the arpeggio between the hands here. We have accepted Mikuli's single arpeggio as more appropriate.

16. Nocturne in E♭ major, op. 55 No. 2

Abbreviations as for Nocturne op. 55 No. 1.

Slurring. FE ends the slur in bar 8 on the note $A\flat^1$ and starts a fresh slur on the dotted minims in bars 20, 22 and 24 (where GE begins a slur from the quaver C^2), as well as at the beginning of the bar in bars 34 and 36 (as in GE). GE does not break the slur in bars 17, 20 or at the beginning of bars 33 and 49. FE and GE do not break the slur at the beginning of bars 32, 35, 43, 51 and 58.

Bar *1*. GE does not indicate *sempre legato*.

Bars *4–5*. FE and GE do not tie the $B\flat^1$ at bars 4–5. We have followed Mikuli's version.

Bar *5*. According to FE and GE, $A\flat^1$ should be played at the beginning of the second half of the bar. We follow the version given by Mikuli. In the original editions the first $A\flat^1$ appears as a minim. We have changed this notation, dividing the minim into a quaver+dotted crotchet in view of the metre. The same applies to bars 31, 32 and 33. In bar 57 the upper $C\flat^3$ is written both in FE and in GE as a minim+dotted quaver.

Bar *10*. GE gives G^1 and not $B\flat^1$ as the sixth quaver in the accompaniment.

Bar *16*. GE gives $E\flat$ and not E as the eighth quaver in the bass.

Bar *25*. GE gives $E\flat^1$ and not D^1 as the second note in the dectuplet.

Bar *27*. The fingering in the bass has been taken from the Oxford edition.

Bar *34*. The original editions do not end the second trill on F^2.

Bar *39*. The original editions do not tie the two $D\flat^2$'s (although they do in bar 13). We have followed Mikuli's version.

Bars *44–45*. GE ties both $D\flat^2$'s at bars 44–45. GE does not tie $A\flat^2$ here but does so in bars 52–53. FE, on the contrary, ties the two $A\flat^2$'s in bars 44–45 but not in bars 52–53.

Bar *46*. GE does not give the dotted minim $A\flat^1$ in the second half of the bar. This note has, however, been added in the later editions.

Bar *47*. The G in the octave at the beginning of the bar is written in GE as a semiquaver, with added semiquaver and crotchet rests.

Bars *52–54*. The trills should, in our opinion, begin on the upper notes.

Bar *55*. In the original editions the acciaccatura $A\flat^1$ is given as an appoggiatura.

17. Nocturne in B major, op. 62 No. 1

Abbreviations: FE – the original French edition (Brandus et Cie, Paris, No. 4611); GE – the original German edition (Breitkopf & Härtel, Leipzig, No. 7547).

The original editions in this work always use a vertical slur to indicate the arpeggio, and not a wavy line. We have retained this peculiarity.

Bar *1*. GE writes the initial arpeggio in small crotchet notes leading to the highest E^2, which is then repeated as a semibreve, the main note. Mikuli gives the same version, but ties the two highest E^2's. In the later issues, GE here agrees with FE.

Bar *4*. In GE, the acciaccatura $A\sharp^1$ is given as an appoggiatura.

Bar *5*. In GE, there is no arpeggio sign before the first chord in the bar.

Bar *6*. In GE, there are not four equal quavers in the top voice at the beginning of the bar, but only two quavers, a dotted quaver and a semiquaver. The same applies to the second half of bar 31.

Bar *8*. In GE, the grace note $D\sharp^1$ is written as a small crotchet note.

Bar *10*. GE gives a crotchet $A\sharp^1$ instead of two consecutive quavers $A\sharp^1$'s.

Bar *12*. FE marks the turn with the customary sign and does not print the notes.

Bar *14*. Chopin gives the third quaver in the bass to the right hand.

Bar *15*. In GE, the last two notes in the treble E^2-$F\sharp^2$ are given as equal quavers.

Bar *17*. The original editions start a new slur at the beginning of this bar and not at the end of the preceding bar.

Bar *31*. In GE, there is no arpeggio sign at the beginning of the bar and $D\sharp^1$ is written in the bass clef.

Bar *34*. FE and GE give the three minims in the chord on one tail in the upper staff (for the right hand alone?) without an arpeggio.

Bar *38*. We have put a dot under the first note in the bass here and in bars 39, 40, 41, 45 and similar bars. GE does not give these dots and FE does not begin them until bar 54.

Bar *42.* In GE, the bass in the first half of the bar is as follows:

In the later issue the same version is given as in FE but without $E\flat$ at the beginning of the bar.

Bar *45.* GE begins a fresh slur from the first quaver in the treble. FE does not break the slur.

Bar *53.* GE ends the slur on the first note in the treble and starts a fresh one on the second. FE does not break the slur at all.

Bar *54.* In GE, the first $A\flat^1$ in the treble is prolonged to the value of a minim, and instead of the following four quavers, given in FE, there are only two, G^1-$G\flat^1$. In the reprint, however, the GE version agrees with that of FE.

Bar *55.* GE has the following version:

Bar *56.* GE does not break the slur in the treble but begins it on the quaver F^1 in bar 55 and ends it on the first $E\flat^2$ in bar 61. We have kept the phrasing of FE, even though this edition gives a different phrasing in the corresponding bars 39—41, which agrees with GE. FE ends the slur on the last note in bar 61.

Bar *62.* In the original editions, the fifth $D\flat^1$-$A\flat^1$ in the bass is written in the upper staff, similarly the G^1 and $G\flat^1$ in the last crotchets in the bass in bars 63—65. It is possible that Chopin intended these top notes to be played with the right hand. It seems more probable, however, that he only meant to simplify the notation.

Bar *64.* In GE, the first $A\flat^2$ in the treble appears over $G\flat$ in the bass and has the value of a dotted crotchet.

Bar *67.* In GE, the first $E\flat^2$ is given as a quaver (coming after a quaver rest), after which the added small note indicates that the trill should begin on $E\flat^2$ (according to FE, in which this note is missing, the trill should begin on the upper $F\flat^2$). In GE the fifth $E\flat$-$B\flat$ in the bass is given in semibreves.

Bar *68.* The small notes given before the main notes in the melody obviously mean that the trills should begin on the latter. In GE they are given as appoggiaturas.

Bar *69.* In GE, there is no E^1 at the beginning of the bar. Contrary to bar 73, FE and GE omit the small note $D\sharp^2$ after the octave leap from $D\sharp^1$ to $D\sharp^2$, probably considering it unnecessary.

Bar *71.* FE has only *rallentando*.

Bars *73—74.* It is uncertain whether the sextuplet in these bars denotes the grouping of three couplets or two triplets.

Bar *75.* GE does not indicate the change of $G\sharp^2$ into G^2 in the trill.

Bar *77.* GE begins the slur on the second quaver ($G\sharp^1$) in the treble, FE on the first quaver but ends the preceding slur on the last note in bar 76.

Bar *79.* Chopin wrote $C\sharp\sharp^2$ instead of D^2 in the last chord in the bar (the chord of the dominant seventh in G$\sharp$ minor is resolved in an interrupted cadence onto the sixth degree, E-$G\sharp$-B, with the added seventh D. This chord, with the augmented root $E\sharp$, is resolved onto $F\sharp$-$A\sharp$-$C\sharp$ at the beginning of bar 80).

Bar *83.* The original editions do not give any sign before the fourteenth semiquaver in the treble. It might be considered that the double sharp in front of the eighth semiquaver applies also to the fourteenth, which is the same note. However, in view of the sign *all'ottava* this double sharp should be repeated. Mikuli distinctly gives a single sharp here.

Bar *84.* Beginning from the fourth semiquaver, the Oxford edition gives the fingering: 1 3 1 3 1 (−) 1 3 1 3 1 4 2.

Bar *85.* FE gives the fingering 1 3 1 2 at the beginning of the bar.

Bar *87.* In FE, there is no E^1 in the chord at the beginning of the second half of the bar.

18. Nocturne in E major, op. 62 No. 2

Abbreviations as for Nocturne op. 62 No 1.

Slurring. In bar 2 FE begins a new slur on the last note in the bar. We have adopted the broader phrasing given in GE; contrary, however, to bar 2, in bar 10 we begin a new slur on the last note in the bar, as in FE and GE. GE does not break the slur in bar 20, nor does FE in bar 21. FE and GE start the slur at the beginning of bar 26 and do not break it in bar 27. In bar 30 GE ends the slur on the first note in the bar, while FE begins the slur on this note. In bar 40 FE and GE start a new slur from the $F\sharp\sharp$, and in bar 41 from the first semiquaver in the bar, without breaking it later in the bar. In bar 43 GE begins a slur on $F\sharp\sharp^1$, which continues until the beginning of bar 47. FE begins the slur on the last crotchet in bar 43 and ends it, as does GE, in bar 47. In bars 49—56 FE gives only two slurs (bars 49—52 and 53—56), while GE gives three (bars 49—50, 51—52 and 53—56). In bar 63 GE does not break the slur. In bar 65 FE and GE end the slur on the first note in the bar. However, a new phrase begins with this $D\sharp^2$ with a variant of the motive:

which continues the sequence. This is why — unlike most recent editions — we begin a new slur on this note. In bar 66 FE begins a new slur on $B\sharp^1$ and in bar 67 on the first A^1. In bar 42 the original editions give two slurs in the lower voice in the bass, each over one half of the bar. We have introduced a slurring which brings out the imitation of the upper voice more clearly. In the bass of the corresponding bar 51, the original editions give one slur over the first half of the bar and two slurs over the second half.

Bars *13* and *16*. In FE, the second crotchet in the bass is given as $F\sharp\text{-}E^1$ only. FE writes the embellishment at the beginning of bar 13 in semiquavers.

Bars *17—18*. In FE, there are *staccato* dots over the crotchets in the bass.

Bar *23*. In GE, there is a B instead of a crotchet rest in the bass.

Bar *24*. In FE, the sign p is indicated directly after the sign sf and not at the beginning of bar 25.

Bar *31*. GE gives A^2 and not $G\sharp^2$ as the seventh note in the run (in small notes).

Bar *35*. The note A in the bass should be taken by the right hand in the second half of the bar.

Bar *37*. In GE, there is no arpeggio sign at the beginning of the bar and the last four semiquavers in the treble are replaced by the quaver E^1 and the semiquavers $F\sharp^1\text{-}F\sharp\sharp^1$. Only in the later issues does GE give a version similar to that in FE, having (erroneously) $D\sharp^1\text{-}E^1$ as quavers instead of semiquavers.

Bar *39*. Instead of a dotted quaver with a semiquaver, GE has two equal quavers at the beginning of the bar in the treble.

Bar *43*. In GE, there is no $D\sharp^1$ in the chord in the treble over the twelfth semiquaver in the bass. GE, probably by an oversight, does not give either of the chords in the right hand at the end of the bar.

Bar *47*. Chopin wrote the chord in this bar with a $B\flat$, using the correct orthography ($A\sharp$) only in bar 48. We have accepted $A\sharp$ in bar 47, by analogy with the $D\sharp$ which in the corresponding phrase he wrote in both bar 56 and bar 57.

Bars *48—49*. At bars 48—49 the harmonic progression moves as follows:

o moll: V   VII[7] ——————— I

In the last chord in bar 48, Chopin wrote $B\sharp$ instead of C^1.

Bar *49*. The semiquaver rests in the bass are our addition. In FE, the third quaver in the middle voices in the right hand is the same as the two preceding quavers, i.e. $G\text{-}C^1$.

Bar *50*. FE does not give D^1 in the chord in the treble over the fourteenth semiquaver in the bass.

Bar *56*. GE gives only $G\sharp$ instead of the quaver thirds $G\sharp\text{-}B$ in the bass.

Bar *58*. The original editions give the last crotchet in the bass as $B\text{-}G\sharp^1$ and not as $B\text{-}E^1\text{-}G\sharp^1$.

Bar *76*. The acciaccatura B is given in GE as an appoggiatura.

19. Nocturne in E minor, op. 72 No. 1

We do not have the original edition by J. Fontana at our disposal and we have therefore taken Mikuli and the Oxford edition as our chief authorities; these in principle repeat the version of the original edition. (This Nocturne is in the thematic index at the beginning of the Oxford edition, corresponding to the complete collection of Chopin's works which was in the possession of Jane Stirling.)

Abbreviation: ME — Mikuli's edition (F. Kistner, Leipzig, No. 5270); OE — the Oxford edition (Oxford University Press).

The slurring, which is very fragmentary in ME and OE, is our addition.

Bar *6*. In the original editions the second crotchet in the treble is given as $F^1\text{-}B^1$ and not as $E\sharp^1\text{-}B^1$. It is not the chord of the dominant seventh ($G\text{-}B\text{-}D\text{-}F$), but the chord of the subdominant seventh in B minor ($E\text{-}G\text{-}B\text{-}D$) with the root augmented ($E\sharp$).

Bar *8*. Recent editions do not repeat $C\sharp^2$ in the melody, but hold it throughout the whole bar as a semibreve. OE gives two tied minim $C\sharp^2$'s. We follow the version given by ME.

Bar *13*. ME, OE and the great majority of other editions tie not only the first two G^1's in the triplet on the second beat of the bar, but also the second and third. We have followed the version given in ME in the repetition, in bar 42, where only the first two G^1's are tied.

Bar *14*. In ME the first note in the melody, D^2, is given not as a dotted minim but as three crotchets tied together, a surprising notation. Klindworth understood it to mean the repetition of D^2 three times, not tying the crotchets, but giving them only a *portamento* slur.

Bar *17*. Recent editions (including OE) give G^1 as the penultimate quaver in the bass. We have $F\sharp^1$, which is in ME and is probably original, since it corresponds with the movement of the bass in the preceding bar (cf. $F^1\text{-}E^1$ and $E^1\text{-}D^1$ in the second and fourth triplets in bar 16 with the corresponding notes in bar 17).

Bar *19*. ME gives E and not B as the eighth quaver in the bass. We have accepted the latter, following OE and recent editions.

Bar *20*. In the melody ME ties the B^1 over to the following bar. OE and recent editions do not have this tie.

Bar 21. The original editions incorrectly write the third and ninth quavers in the bass as *F* instead of *E$\sharp$*.

Bar 23. Most editions, including OE, indicate *aspiramente*, which is not given in ME.

Bar 24. In the majority of recent editions the last crotchet in the bar is given as *A^1-C^2*. We have followed the ME and OE version, with *C$\sharp$* instead of *C*. Similarly in bar 48 we give the analogous *D^2-F$\sharp^2$* from ME.

Bar 26. In ME and OE, the note *B^1* in the treble has the value of an undotted minim and the third *D$\sharp^2$-F$\sharp^2$* that of a dotted minim. We have made the version given in this bar uniform with that of bar 30.

Bars 32—33. It is difficult to decide whether the sextuplets in these bars form three groups of two notes or two groups of three. In Chopin we find the sextuplet sign given indiscriminately for both these combinations.

Bars 47—48. Some editions introduce a version in the treble similar to that in bars 23—24. We have followed the version given in ME (and in OE in bar 47), which is apparently authentic.

Bar 55. In OE the two chords in the treble are tied, i.e. the second chord should not be played. This version, probably taken from Fontana's edition, is obviously erroneous. Some editions (Kleczyński, Pugno, Brugnoli) give only one chord having the value of a semibreve. We have the version given by Mikuli and Klindworth.

COMMENTARY: *Polonaises*

1. Polonaise in C♯ minor, op. 26 No. 1

Abbreviations: FE — the original French edition (M. Schlesinger, Paris, No. 1929); GE — the original German edition (Breitkopf & Härtel, Leipzig, No. 5707).

Bar 1. FE indicates only *Appassionato.*

Bar 8. The last note in the left hand, $G\sharp^1$, is placed in both FE and GE on the upper staff, perhaps in order to emphasize that it should be played with the right hand.

Bars 9—10, 21—22 etc. We reproduce the short slurs in the treble from FE and GE, which have them at bars 46—47.

Bar 11. In FE the grace note $F\sharp^2$ has no stroke, as at bar 23. Yet at bar 48, in FE, it has. GE has a stroke consistently.

Bar 12. FE and GE have no slur in the left hand, as at bar 24. At bar 49 only the notes $F\sharp^1$ and E^1 are slurred.

Bars 35—36. In FE and GE the phrase slur ends at bar 35 and a new one starts at the beginning of bar 36.

Bar 42. At the beginning of the bar FE indicates *forte* (*f*), and next to it *sforzato* (*sf*). GE has *fortissimo* (*ff*).

Bars 51 and **83.** In FE and GE the turn is notated as follows:

i.e. both these editions connect it with the F^1 which precedes the turn in the middle part. But this note certainly cannot belong to the melody, or Chopin would have written the first note of the upper part as a dotted crotchet, and not as a minim. We therefore follow recent editions in replacing it by Ab^1 and tying it to the preceding note. Chopin probably used the above-mentioned notation (the simplest even though inaccurate) to emphasize that the turn should be played only after the fourth quaver in the bar, and not at the same time as it. This means that the turn must be understood as a sextuplet without the first note:

or, which we consider much better, as a triplet:

Bar 53. FE and GE write the grace notes as quavers. In bar 85 FE also marks them as quavers, unlike GE which has semiquavers.

Bars 54 and **86.** The same remarks apply to the notation of the turn as at bars 51 and 83. At bar 86 FE ties the Db^2 at the end of the turn to the Db^2 in the following chord. GE does not have this tie. At bar 54 neither edition has it.

Bars 66—69. FE and GE extend the slur in the bass to the end of bar 66 and to the Gb^1 in bar 68. In the same editions, in bars 67 and 69, the bass has a separate slur. Bars 66—69 are harmonically indefinite. They are based on the chord of the diminished seventh. Yet these four bars are immediately repeated in sequence a semitone lower (bars 70—73) with a strong flavour of C minor, and are written accordingly (B-D-F-Ab — VII^7 in C minor, which at bar 73 changes enharmonically to VII^7 in Eb major). They should therefore be understood as being in Db major (which, since the preceding passage ends in this key, is the most natural interpretation). Thus the principal chord in this passage should be notated C-Eb-Gb-Bb. We have altered the notation of FE and GE in such a way that the treble in bars 66—69 has Bbb instead of A, which seems to be the most rational solution. Nevertheless Chopin seems to have understood this chord as being VII^7 in Bb minor — at any rate he wrote it as such (A-C-Eb-Gb with its natural resolution to Bb-Db-F); yet in bar 68 he inconsistently writes the fifth semiquaver in the bass as Bbb instead of A.

Bar 77. Recent editions give a flat to the C^2 in the treble at the beginning of the bar. This is not found in FE, GE or Mikuli's edition. At the beginning of this bar Mikuli restores a flat beside the A^1, which, in the preceding bar, has a natural. It may be that this flat was erroneously added to the C^2. It must be admitted, however, that the Cb^2 is perfectly possible. GE has no *f* in the bass, unlike FE and Mikuli's edition, where this marking was possibly given in error instead of *sf*.

Bar 79. FE and GE do not have the flat over the mordent. Cb^2 is given only in recent editions. C^2, however, seems more appropriate.

Bar 97. The repeat of the main section of the polonaise after the trio is not marked in either FE or GE. Moreover, both editions clearly indicate *Fine* at bar 97. It may be imagined, however, that this is a misprint. There is not the slightest reason to suppose that Chopin wanted to abandon the principle, which he observed in all the other polonaises, of repeating the main part of the work (at least in a shortened form and occasionally with changes) after the trio. Mikuli's edition has *Da capo*, which we reproduce here.

2. Polonaise in E♭ minor, op. 26 No. 2

Abbreviations as for Polonaise op. 26 No. 1.

Bar 10. According to Mikuli, Chopin changed the flats before $D♭^2$ and $D♭^3$ into naturals with his own hand. This correction was made in the copy belonging to his pupil, Madame Rubio. GE has D in this run consistently.

Bar 11. FE does not tie the $G♭^3$'s in the treble. We reproduce FE's slurring of the corresponding bar 115. In other repetitions of this bar FE begins the slur either on the first semiquaver or on the crotchet in the treble. GE always starts the slur on the crotchet.

Bars 13—14 and 17—18. FE and GE end the slur on the fourth semiquaver in the treble, as in the subsequent repetitions of these bars. Moreover, GE (always) and FE (usually) begin the slur in these bars not on the semiquaver $B♭$, but on the preceding crotchet, $C♭$. For the last quaver in the left hand at bar 13 GE has $B♭$-$E♭^1$-G^1, as at bar 14. The same applies to the subsequent repetitions of this passage.

Bars 18, 66 and similar bars. Chopin wrongly wrote E^1 in the last chord in the bass instead of $F♭^1$ (the chord VII⁷ in A♭ minor).

Bars 35—36. FE ties the two bottom F's in the bass over the bar-line instead of slurring the notes E-F (which it does in bars 33—34). This would mean that the F at the beginning of bar 36 should not be played. The same applies to the corresponding bar in the recapitulation. However, this is probably a misprint.

Bar 38. Instead of the seventh $B♭$-$A♭^1$ at the end of the bar in the right hand GE has an octave $A♭$-$A♭^1$, as in the corresponding bar in the recapitulation (142).

Bar 73. Although at bar 69 Chopin wrote the last chord correctly, with $C\text{\#\#}^1$, yet both here and at bar 77 he wrote D^1 instead.

Bars 81—82 and 89—90. The A is given first to the right hand (bars 81—82) and then to the left hand (bars 89—90). This is probably accidental. Recent editions have introduced a uniform notation.

Bar 94. GE has B instead of $A\#$ in the last chord in the treble, which was perhaps intentional in a work that so abounds in variants.

Bar 97. In the copy belonging to Chopin's sister, Madame Jędrzejewicz, the *pp* before the tremolo is crossed out in pencil, and may even be replaced by *ff*.

Bars 103—104. In FE and GE the first octave in the left hand at bar 103 is written, obviously unintentionally, as $F\#$-$F\#$. (GE shows only the upper notes and not the lower octaves in the bass of bars 103—104.) Mikuli's edition has the octave $_1G\#$-$G\#$.

Bar 125. In FE the lower F is missing from the chord at the beginning of the bar.

Bars 147—148. FE does not tie the $E♭^1$'s over the bar-line; it does tie them, however, in the corresponding bars 43-44.

Bar 175. In the copy belonging to Madame Jędrzejewicz, FE's *ppp* is crossed out and replaced by *ff* (cf. the note on bar 97). The same change was made in Jane Stirling's copy (cf. E. Ganche: *Voyages avec F. Chopin*, Paris 1934, page 144). Both GE and FE have *ppp*.

3. Polonaise in A major, op. 40 No. 1

Abbreviations: M — the autograph, according to the reproduction in L. Binental's book *Chopin. Life and Art of the Composer* (Warsaw 1937, plate XII); FE — the original French edition (E. Troupenas et Cᶦᵉ, Paris, No. 977); GE — the original German edition (Breitkopf & Härtel, Leipzig, No. 6331). As GE agrees with M, it may be presumed to have been based on the autograph.

Bar 1. M has *ff*.

Bar 3. In the last chord of the right hand in this bar M and GE have $C\#^1$ instead of D^1; and in the left hand they have A instead of B (i.e. these notes are repeated from the preceding chords). The same occurs in all subsequent repetitions. We reproduce FE's version. M and GE indicate a fresh pedal for the last four semiquavers in this bar. At bar 1, however, they do not have corresponding pedal-marks. FE gives no pedalling at all in this polonaise.

Bar 7. GE starts the slur on the first note of the bar, and ends it on the last. FE does not have it at all. M starts a slur on the second note of the treble and ends it on the last.

Bars 9, 10, 13, 14. In contrast to the similar bars 2 and 4, M and GE hold the pedal until the penultimate quaver.

Bar 11. Both here and at bar 75 FE has $B\#^1$ instead of $C\#^2$ in the fifth chord in the right hand.

Bar 12. In the second chord in the right hand recent editions omit the $C\#^3$ for the sake of easier execution. We have retained the version of M, FE and GE. In the corresponding chords at bars 13, 14 and 78, M and the original editions have no $C\#^3$. In the bass of bar 12 FE has the bare octave $G\#$-$G\#$, as also at bar 76.

Bar 13. FE has $C\#^2$-$D\#^2$-$F\#\#^2$-$A\#^2$ as the second and third chords in the right hand of this bar. FE adds $A\#^1$. We have followed the version of M and GE, which corresponds to the chords in bar 14.

Bar 25. FE does not have the *energico* that is marked in M and GE.

Bars 25—26. M, FE and GE phrase these bars with one slur, as in the following two bars. At bars 35—36 they give the phrasing which we have accepted for both passages.

Bar 29. Instead of the single *B* at the beginning of the bar, which we have taken from M, GE and Mikuli's edition, and which is generally accepted, FE has the full chord:

It is possible that Chopin introduced this chord at the proof stage of FE. The same applies to bar 53.

Bar 31. FE writes out the repeat of this section in full: at the bar corresponding to bar 31, it adds an A^2 to the second, third, fourth and seventh chords. M and GE also write it out in full, but add the *A* only to the first chord of this and the two corresponding bars. In the penultimate chord in the treble of bar 31, M has A^2 instead of $F\sharp^2$.

Bar 32. Here and at bar 56 M and GE hold the pedal throughout the whole bar.

Bar 33. In this bar and its subsequent repetitions M and GE shorten the first octave in the treble from a minim to a crotchet, separating it from the following octave by a crotchet rest.

Bar 34. In the semiquaver chords in the bass of this bar and its subsequent repetitions M and GE add an *A* between the $F\sharp$ and D^1.

Bar 35. In FE the last two chords in the bass are given here and in the repetitions of this bar as *B-D-A*, as at bar 27.

Bars 37—40. In these bars FE has fuller chord. For the bass it gives the version which we preserve here (except for the second chord in the bass of bar 40, which is an exact repetition of the first). However, in the treble of bar 37 it gives the last three chords an additional F^2; and similarly the last three chords of bar 38 have a G^2:

In FE bars 39—40 are as follows:

The notation of the right hand in M and GE is the same as that given here, with the exception of the first chord of bar 37, where we have retained FE's $E\flat^2$, and of the penultimate chord of bar 40, where we retain FE's A^3. M and GE do not give the $E\flat^1$'s and D^1 in the left-hand part of bar 37, nor the F^1's and E^1 in bar 38. At bar 40 FE does not tie either of the A^1's in the last two chords in the bass. All these remarks apply also to bars 61—64.

Bars 41 and 43. M and GE mark the demisemiquavers here staccato, while at bars 45 and 46 they give the semiquavers legato slurs. FE gives no marks

at all. Mikuli's edition slurs the demisemiquavers as well.

Bar 45. FE gives the third semiquaver as *F*.

Bar 46. GE gives the semiquavers at the end of the bar as: $C\sharp$-*D*-*E*-$F\sharp$. This is probably a misprint. We follow the version of M and FE.

Bar 48. As written, the transition from the last trill to the first notes of bar 49 is rather clumsy and unsatisfactory. It would be advisable to link it this way:

i.e. by adding a further grace-note, *D*, an octave below the existing one (which is shown in M, FE and GE).

The last bar. M and GE indicate *fff*.

4. Polonaise in C minor, op. 40 No. 2

Abbreviations as for Polonaise op. 40 No. 1.

Bar 3. In GE, the third and fourth chords in the right hand are the same as the first two, i.e. *G*-C^1-$E\flat^1$-G^1. In this bar, as in bars 5, 11, 13 and similar, GE does not start the slur in the bass until the second octave. FE either has no slurs in these bars or begins the slur on the second beat of the bar (e.g. bar 11). Only in one instance does it agree with GE.

Bar 7. For the first chord in the treble GE has C^1-$A\flat^1$-C^2 — i.e. the same as the following chord, and also the same as subsequent repetitions of this bar.

Bar 10. GE does not have the G^1 on the penultimate quaver in the treble either here or in repetitions of this bar.

Bar 11. GE begins this bar and its repetitions thus:

FE, both here and at the beginning of bar 48, has only the sixth $E\flat^1$-C^2.

Bar 14. In FE the fourth chord in the treble is an exact repeat of the preceding one, both here and in repetitions of this bar.

Bar 18. After this bar, FE and GE repeat bars 1—18, printing them in full, but without the *sotto voce*. GE even adds *forte*.

Bars 19 and 21. We advise playing the octave $A\flat$-$A\flat^1$ with both thumbs.

Bars 21—22. FE ties the C^2's over the bar-line. However it does not tie bars 19—20.

Bar 26. GE begins the *diminuendo* at this bar.

Bar 27. GE has only $F\sharp^2$ for the eighth semiquaver.

Bars 27—33. The notation of FE and GE, which we follow, does not bring out the melody in this passage sufficiently clearly. In our opinion, the melody should be indicated in the following way:

Bars *28—29*. GE ties the lower *G*'s over the barline.

Bar *31*. FE has only E^1 for the ninth semiquaver.

Bar *35*. FE and GE write the dotted crotchet *B* in the upper staff, giving it to the right hand.

Bars *36—40*. Except for the quaver rest in bar 36, all the rests in the treble staff in bars 36—39 are missing in FE and GE, as is also the quaver rest at the start of bar 40.

Bar *40*. At the beginning of the bar in the left hand FE has only the upper *C*'s.

Bar *57*. The chord at the end of this bar is identical to the one at the beginning of the following bar. It is the minor subdominant with augmented first and with an added augmented sixth, between two chords of the tonic in A♭ major. In bar 58 Chopin notates it with *B* and *D*. However at bar 57 he writes $C♭^1$ and *E♭♭*, thus unnecessarily complicating the notation.

Bars *62—63*. Both here and at bar 89 GE ties the last G^1 in the treble to the preceding, and not to the following, G^1, which latter note, indeed, it does not give at all. Our notation follows FE. In the second chord of bars 63 and 90, GE has not $D♭^1$-$A♭^1$-$D♭^2$, but $D♭^1$-F^1-$D♭^2$.

Bar *66*. FE gives the fifth quaver, $E♭^1$, to the right hand, as at bar 93. The *A*'s in the left hand are tied in FE at bar 66, but not at bar 93.

Bar *70*. FE repeats the $E♭^1$ on the second quaver of the bar simultaneously with the sixth C^2.

Bars *71—81*. FE slurs the second half of bar 71 and the whole of bar 72 and then starts a new slur at bar 73, continuing it as far as the beginning of bar 75. It then has one slur from the second half of bar 75 to the first note of bar 77, after which another runs from the $D♭^1$ in bar 77 to the beginning of bar 81; a new slur then starts on the third crotchet of bar 81. GE only slurs bars 71—72 and 75—76 as far as the ends of bars 72 and 76 respectively. At the beginning of bar 73 it starts a new slur, which ends on the first *G* in the melody. The

slur which GE starts at the beginning of bar 77 ends on the last note of bar 82.

Bar *73*. FE does not mark the "arpeggio" sign.

Bars *79—80*. These bars should be notated as follows:

Bars *97—100*. FE and GE differ greatly in the notation of these bars. We have accepted GE's version, but replacing the minim $B♭^1$ in the top part in bar 98 by the two crotchets $B♭^1$-$A♭^1$ that are found in FE. The latter repeats the $E♭^1$ on the second quaver of bar 97 (cf. the note on bar 70). For the second quaver of bar 98 it has the chord $D♭^1$-G^1-C^2 (having begun the bar on $D♭^1$ and not C^1). For the second quaver of bar 99 it has the chord C^1-D^1-$B♭^1$; and in the left hand at the beginning of the bar it has a crotchet *F* (the upper octave of the last semiquaver of bar 98).

Bars *108—109*. GE does not tie the G^1's over the bar-line.

5. Polonaise in F♯ minor, op. 44

Abbreviations: FE — the original French edition (M. Schlesinger, Paris, No. 3477); GE — the original German edition (P. Mechetti, Vienna, No. 3577).

Bars *4—5*. In FE and GE the middle one of the three *D*'s on the last semiquaver of bar 4 and the first of bar 5 is given to the right hand. We have given it to the left hand, as Chopin himself did further on at bar 5 (eighth and ninth semiquavers).

Bars *5—8*. FE and GE mark no phrasing. (This work in general contains very few dynamic and rhythmic markings in the original editions.) In the corresponding passage before the recapitulation FE has one slur over bars 264—265, and a second over bars 266—267. GE covers all these four bars with one slur.

Bar *18*. FE and GE do not give the ending of the trill here, though they do in corresponding subsequent bars. Together with the quavers $E♯$-*B* repeated four times, FE has also four $C♯$'s (the lower octave of the $C♯$ in the melody). The same occurs in the later corresponding bars.

Bar *23*. GE does not have the *D* in the first chord in the left hand. In the following bar it also lacks the *D* in the first octave of the triplet in both hands. The corresponding subsequent bars are still less exact in such details.

Bars *27—33*. In these bars and in the subsequent corresponding bars, the markings of the "arpeggio" signs before the octave in FE and GE are very irregular.

Bar *28*. In FE the last quaver in the left hand is the same as the preceding one: F-C^1-$E♭^1$-F^1, as at bar 54.

B a r *29.* In GE the octave *F¹-F²* is shortened both here and at bar 55 to a demisemiquaver, as is the octave *E♭¹-E♭²* at bar 33.

B a r *31.* Both here and in subsequent corresponding passages the first octave in the right hand is notated in GE as follows:

B a r *31.* Both here and in subsequent corresponding passages the first octave in the right hand is notated in GE as follows:

This notation is presumably equivalent to the notation which is given in the present edition and reproduced from bars 57 and 290 in FE. At bar 31 FE ties the grace note to the principal note, which would indicate an octave spread downwards without a grace note (Mikuli, in his edition, also has this notation at bars 31 and 57, but not at bar 290). At bar 107 FE does not have the "arpeggio" sign before the octave — probably owing to an oversight. In view of the grace note before the upper note of the octave (unlike the octaves at bars 27, 29 and 33, where the lower note has a grace note) it is not certain whether at bar 31 and similar bars the octave should be spread downwards after the grace note or not.

B a r *32.* The second octave in the treble, *D♭¹-D♭²*, is notated in FE as a semiquaver and not a demisemiquaver.

B a r *35 et seq.* In FE, the upper notes of the octaves in the treble which should be held longer than a quaver have additional crotchet tails besides the quaver tails; similarly later on, at bar 61 et seq. Chopin, however, meant the lower notes to be lengthened also, as may be seen from the fact that in bars 37, 38, and similar bars not only the upper note of the octave but also the lower one have dots. Here and in the later corresponding passages we have accepted GE's notation, and have applied the same principles also at bars 13—14.

B a r *36.* FE has the fourth quaver in this bar as *D-F♯¹-D¹*, i.e. the *B* is missing.

B a r *37.* In GE the penultimate quaver in the left hand has an additional *F♯* between the *D* and the *G♯*.

B a r *43.* In FE and GE the beginning of the bar runs as follows:

In FE and GE the phrasing varies both here and in the later repetitions of this bar. The slur begins sometimes on the first right-hand chord in the bar, sometimes on the semiquaver immediately following, and sometimes on the crotchet *A¹* on the second beat of the bar. We have accepted the last version as the one that best suits the appropriate articulation.

B a r s *61—64.* The notes in the run in the bass should be played as if they had been notated as demisemiquavers, thus:

B a r s *61—64.* The notes in the run in the bass should be played as if they had been notated as demisemiquavers, thus:

B a r s *94* and *118.* GE has the last octave as in the preceding bar, i.e. *E-E*, and not *C-C*.

B a r s *96* and *120.* The last octave is notated in GE as in the preceding bar, i.e. *F-F*, and not *D-D*.

B a r s *98* and *122.* In the demisemiquaver group Chopin writes *E♭-C♭*, and not *D♯-B*, introducing an enharmonic change from *E♭* to *D♯* only at the end of the bar (the chord is the subdominant in A minor with an added sixth *B* and the root sharpened from *D* to *D♯*).

B a r *122.* GE has *C* instead of *C♭* (which we have changed to *B*, cf. the note on bar 98).

B a r *127 et seq.* Only this trio has any pedal-marks in FE. In FE and GE there is no phrasing in the bass at bars 129—138, nor at bars 149—158.

B a r *132.* In GE the *C♯¹* is missing from the chord in the left hand on the third beat of the bar.

B a r *143.* GE has *C♯²* instead of *D²* at the beginning of the bar, as at bar 163, where there is *G♯²* instead of *A²*.

B a r *155.* FE has only *B* for the second crotchet in the bass.

B a r *165.* FE and GE start a slur in this bar, which continues until bar 176.

B a r *171.* In the left hand FE and GE have *F¹* and not *E♯¹* at the beginning of the bar. We prefer a simpler notation analogous to that used by Chopin at bars 175, 230 and 234.

B a r *178.* In FE and GE the slur that begins in this bar is continued as far as bar 184.

B a r *181.* FE has no mordent.

B a r s *218—219.* In GE these bars run as follows:

B a r *232.* FE and GE end the slur that begins in this bar on the last crotchet of bar 239.

B a r *234.* In GE the last two notes in both hands are equal quavers.

B a r *240.* FE has no mordent.

B a r *241.* GE ties the upper *B*'s in the left hand. FE does not tie the minim *B* in the bass to the *B* in the following bar.

B a r s *250—251* and *258—259.* This run consists of the notes of the dominant chord in F♯ minor, *C♯-E♯-G♯*, each preceded by the note a semitone lower – i.e. $B\sharp$, $D\sharp\sharp$ and $F\sharp\sharp$. FE and GE write E instead of $D\sharp\sharp$.

Bar 270. GE has an additional $F\sharp^1$ in the chord on the penultimate quaver in the left hand.

Bar 294. In the second chord on the second beat of the bar, FE has as well as E^1-A^1-E^2 a $C\sharp^2$, which is tied to the $C\sharp^2$ in the preceding chord.

Bars 314–315. Klindworth rightly considers the first notes of the chromatic scale, $D\sharp$-E, as the ending of the left-hand trill. He also divides the chromatic scale so that there are four notes to each of the right hand's quavers.

Bar 320. In FE the second quaver of this bar differs from that of the subsequent bars in being a repetition of the preceding chord, i.e. it has the $F\sharp$ as well as the $C\sharp$ and A.

Bars 323–324. FE does not tie the $C\sharp^1$ in the right hand.

6. Polonaise in A♭ major, op. 53

Abbreviations: FE – the original French edition (M. Schlesinger, Paris, No. 3958); GE – the original German edition (Breitkopf & Härtel, Leipzig, No. 7002).

Bar 5. FE does not have the $A\flat$ in the left hand in the first chord of the bar.

Bar 12. FE does not have the D^1 in the second chord of the bar.

Bar 14. We have retained the notation of FE and GE, though the following would be more appropriate:

In this way the melodic progression $B\flat^1$-C^2-$D\flat^2$ is emphasized.

Bars 16–17. We follow GE's phrasing. FE continues the slur as far as the end of bar 16.

Bar 26. GE has the following at the end of this bar and bar 42:

At bars 74 and 164 it has a semiquaver and a quaver, with no rest between them.

Bar 28. FE and GE have no C^1 in the last chord of the bar.

Bars 33, 34, 37, 38 and *similar bars.* The grace note before the trill is given only to indicate that the trill should begin on the principal note ($E\flat^1$ or F^1).

Bar 36. FE has no "arpeggio" sign before the second chord in the treble either here or at bars 68 and 158.

Bars 44 and 76. FE has no C^1 in the last chord in the bass.

Bar 47. FE does not break the slur either here or at bar 79.

Bar 48. FE and GE have no "arpeggio" sign before the penultimate chord. FE, unlike GE, does have it at bar 80.

Bars 50–51 and **54–55.** The C^2 in the right-hand part is tied in FE between bars 50 and 51. GE does not have this tie. In the similar passage at bars 54–55 FE slurs the $E\flat^2$ and the G^2, while GE ties the two $E\flat^2$'s. We think that in each case Chopin intended to tie the note common to both chords.

Bars 58–59. It is clear from bars 62 and 63, where a grace note an octave lower precedes the trill, and where the trill should then begin on the principal note $D\flat^2$, that the trill at bars 58–59 should be executed in the same way. All the trills in these bars should probably end in the same way as the first in the original editions (bar 64). FE (like Mikuli's edition) has F-G for the last quaver in the left hand at bars 58 and 59, and not F-$A\flat$.

Bar 64. FE has no $B\flat$ in the second chord, nor does it have the $E\flat^3$ at the end of the run. In GE this run begins only after the last chord; in FE it starts on the penultimate chord of the bar.

Bar 65. FE does not have ff.

Bars 81–82. In FE the "arpeggio" sign is continuous, probably because the two bottom notes in the right-hand chords are written on the lower staff and are therefore linked with the chord in the bass. In GE the right-hand chords are written on the upper staff and each hand has a separate "arpeggio" sign as at bars 101–102 and 180. At bar 100 both editions place the right-hand chords on the lower staff, and therefore do not break the "arpeggio" signs.

Bar 83. FE has one p, though at bar 103 it has pp.

Bar 90. FE does not break the slur. GE breaks it at the end of the bar. At bar 110 FE does not break the slur; GE has the slurring accepted here.

Bar 92. In FE the semiquaver $C\sharp^1$ in the right hand has no leger line, but hangs in mid-air. But it is placed higher than the following B, and cannot be meant to be the same. The same applies to bar 112. Some recent editions, however, have taken this note to be another B.

Bar 96. FE ends one slur on the second semiquaver, and starts a new slur on the third semiquaver in the right hand. GE starts a new slur on the second semiquaver.

Bar 124. FE and GE start a new slur on the last crotchet of bar 124 instead of at the beginning of bar 125.

Bar 130. FE has no mordent on the G^1.

Bar 134. GE has no mordent.

Bar 141. In FE the last two notes in the right hand are equal semiquavers, as in the similar bar 133 in both FE and GE. In GE the $B\flat^2$ is notated as a demisemiquaver followed by a demisemiquaver rest, so that the A^2 is a semiquaver. We have accepted Mikuli's version. Recent editions have accepted one or other of these rhythms, introducing a corresponding change in bar 133; e.g. Klindworth, in both these passages, has the rhythm , where Brugnoli has  .

Bars 148 and *150*. GE has naturals before the *E*'s at the beginning of these bars, as at bars 149 and 151. FE has *E♭* at bars 148 and 150 and *E* at bars 149 and 151. This version is more appropriate, since the *E♭* in bars 148 and 150 corresponds to the same note in bars 144 and 146, while at bars 149 and 151 *E* corresponds to the *E¹* in the treble of bars 145 and 147.

Bar *170*. In GE the *C¹* is missing from the fourth chord in the left hand.

Bar *173*. GE writes *B* instead of *C♭¹* in the chord on the third quaver in the bass, although it had *C♭¹* at bar 171.

Bar *175*. Klindworth brings out the main theme in the chords more clearly, as follows:

7. *Polonaise-Fantasia, op. 61*

Abbreviations: FE — the original French edition (Brandus et Cⁱᵉ, Paris, No. 4610); **GE** — the original German edition (Breitkopf & Härtel, Leipzig, No. 7546).

Bar *3*. GE has not *f* but *pp*.

Bar *5*. GE has an *E♭* in the right-hand chord instead of a *D♭*, but still ties it to the *D♭* in the preceding bar. This is probably a misprint.

Bar *7*. In GE the *D♭* is missing from the second chord.

Bar *10*. GE does not tie the octave *C♭-C♭¹* at the end of this bar over the bar-line.

Bar *20*. FE has *B♯* as the last note in the bass and not *B*, as given in GE. This *B♯* may be authentic, especially in view of the *B♯* in the first chord of the following bar.

Bar *25*. In the third chord in the bass GE has *F¹* instead of *E♭¹*. This is probably a misprint, for in the repetition of this passage at bar 45 both GE and FE have *E♭¹*.

Bars *25* and *29*. FE and GE do not make it clear that the semiquavers in these bars are to be played with the right hand.

Bar *31*. For the last semiquaver in the treble FE has not just *A♭²*, but the chord *C²-E♭²-A♭²*, as at the beginning of the following bar. According to the original editions, the last quaver in the left hand is the sixth *F¹-D♭²*, without the *B♭¹*. This is probably an inadvertent omission. FE and GE do not break the slur in this bar.

Bar *33*. FE and GE start a new slur at the beginning of the bar. GE has *G¹* and not *A♭¹* in the chord at the beginning of the bar.

Bar *36*. GE not only has no natural before the *G¹* in the chord on the third quaver, but adds a flat before the *G²*. According to GE, the fourth quaver in the right hand is an *F²* without the lower sixth *A♭¹*. GE has no *G* in the left-hand part in the chord on the last quaver in the bar.

Bars *41–42*. FE and GE do not break the slurs either at the beginning of these bars or at bar 43.

Bar *45*. In contrast to bar 25, the fourth quaver in the bass in GE has the seventh *D♭¹* as well as the octave *E♭-E♭¹*. This makes it match bar 44.

Bar *46*. FE and GE begin a new slur on the last note in the right hand.

Bars *52–53*. We have accepted the notation of recent editions. In FE and GE, the ninth semiquaver in the right hand at bar 52 is *C♯²-E²* and the eleventh *D♯²-F♯²*. Similarly at bar 53 the eighth semiquaver is *D♯²-F♯²*.

Bar *55*. The fingering of the left hand comes from FE and GE.

Bars *56–61*. The subtle harmonic progression in these bars, when reduced to its basic shape, appears as a kind of transitional passage between the chords *E♭-G-B♭* at the beginning of bar 56 and *E♭-G-B♭-D♭* at the beginning of bar 61. This insertion is basically a sequence of dominant seventh — tonic progressions falling a tone each time, i.e. in A♭ major, G♭ major, F♭ major and E♭ major.

Pattern I

Pattern II

In FE and GE the second chord is not V⁷ but VII (in A♭ major) with a diminished seventh and diminished third: *G-B♭♭-D♭-F♭*. Chopin notates it as *B♭♭-D♭-F♭-A♭♭*, i.e. V⁷ in E♭♭ major, in order to simplify it and so make it easier to read. He changes the *A♭♭* to *G* only at the end of bar 57 in chord 3, which is the same chord, but contains anticipations in the shape of the *C* and the *E♭*. (Where the identical chord occurs in bar 56 these are only changing notes.) Chopin further adds a minor seventh to chords 4 and 6, so that chords 4, 5, 6 and 7 form a series of dominant sevenths that proceed through the circle of fifths, but are further altered in that the fifth in chords 4 and 6 is flattened. Pattern II shows the chords in their final form as given in FE and GE. But Chopin writes *D* instead of *E♭♭* in chord 4, and *C* and *E* instead of *D♭♭* and *F♭* in chord 6.

B a r *61*. In GE and Mikuli's edition the grace note *A♭¹* is tied to the same note immediately following. If the version without this tie is accepted, it is advisable to spread the octave.

B a r s *67—69*. FE and GE do not tie the *D♭¹*'s over the bar-line. Yet at bars 73—75 they tie the corresponding *A♭*'s, and at bars 81—83 the *A*'s.

B a r *78*. Here and towards the end of the preceding bar, GE unnecessarily changes the notation of the *E♮* to *F♭²*, returning to *E²* at bar 79.

B a r *92*. The last two quavers in the bass are notated in GE as *B♭-A♭*, (and not *A♭-B♭*, as in FE); similarly the fifth and sixth quavers at bar 93.

B a r *100*. In FE the last two notes of the melody are equal quavers. GE's version is retained in the present edition, except that the last note in the bass, the *A♭*, is a semiquaver (parallelling the rhythm of the melody) and is linked by an upper ligature to the preceding *G♭*.

B a r *101*. The phrasing is reproduced from FE and GE.

B a r *103*. GE does not tie the two *D¹*'s at the beginning of the bar. The chord of the diminished seventh, which in the preceding bars can be interpreted in various ways, becomes at bar 103 VII⁷ in *G♭* minor (or *G♭* major) and as such ought to be notated with an *E♭♭* and not a *D*. For this reason we have changed the original notation. The last note in the bass is given in GE as *D♭¹* and not *E♭¹*.

B a r s *103—107*. The frequent combinations of two rhythms, , are notated in FE with the semiquaver immediately over the third quaver in the triplet. GE has the corresponding semiquavers after the third note of the triplets. Yet in bars 109—115, where similar combinations of two rhythms often occur, GE puts the semiquavers immediately over the third quavers of the triplets.

B a r s *108—115*. In this passage FE and GE do not sufficiently clearly and consistently distinguish the upper part in the right hand, which contains the melody, from the lower notes which fill in the harmony. We have made appropriate changes, in the main following Scholtz' edition (C. F. Peters, Leipzig).

B a r *125*. FE does not tie the *G²* at the beginning of the bar to the one at the end of the preceding bar. Yet it ties the two *F²*'s immediately following. There is no *tr.* sign over the eighth semiquaver.

B a r *126*. GE has the octave *G-G* in the left hand at the beginning of the bar. For the last quaver it has the octave *B♭-B♭¹*, not the sixth *B♭-G¹*.

B a r *127*. The left hand in GE is in equal quavers, with the same chord on the third quaver as is given for the second, fourth and fifth.

B a r *131*. The chord which at bars 128—129 took the form *C♯-E-G-B♭* resolves at bar 132 into the triad *B-D-F♯*, and is therefore re-notated as *A♯-C♯-E-G*. The notation in FE and GE does not make this enharmonic change clear, as we have. In the same bar FE has no octave *G-G* in the left hand.

B a r *135*. According to B. Wójcik-Keuprulian (*Melodyka Chopina*, Lwów 1930, p. 24) the grace note in this bar should not exceed the value of a semiquaver in duration. J. P. Dunn (*Ornamentation in the Works of Fred. Chopin*, p. 42) gives this note a theoretic crotchet value, though agreeing that it should be played as a quaver. We favour the latter view, on the grounds that if Chopin had wanted to give it only the value of a semiquaver he would have notated it as a small quaver with no stroke through it. By writing it as a small crotchet, however, he obviously intended to prolong it, which is consistent with the pathetic character of this passage.

B a r *137*. GE gives the bass as follows:

B a r *148*. GE has only *più lento*.

B a r *165*. The third chord in this bar should really have *D♯♯* instead of *E*, since it is VII of V in a progression (in *A♯* major) I — VII⁷ of V — VII⁷ — I. But as it may be understood as a passing chord, we have left the original notation.

B a r *167*. FE and GE write the third quaver as *D*, and not *C♯♯*, as it should be.

B a r *173*. GE has no crotchet *F♯¹* on the second beat of the bar.

B a r *174*. FE has *F♯-C♯¹* for the last quaver in the left hand and not *A-C♯¹*.

B a r *176*. GE has *B¹* alone, without the *F♯¹*, in the right hand at the beginning of the bar.

B a r s *182—185*. The bass in GE lacks the richness of ours, running:

B a r *188*. In GE the *C♯¹* is missing from the chord on the third quaver from the end of the bar.

B a r s *200, 202* and *204*. The third beat of the bar consists of three groups of two semiquavers rather than two groups of three (i.e. the effect is of a trill that is getting faster). It is thus in fact a quaver triplet broken into semiquavers.

B a r s *209* and *212*. In GE the grace note, *A♯*, is a quaver with a stroke through the tail. We reproduce the longer grace note from FE. In our opinion, it should have the value of a quaver, as at bar 135.

A semiquaver would introduce too violent a rhythm, not suited to this quiet, dreamy passage. On the other hand, a crotchet grace note would overemphasize its resolution, i.e. the *B* in the inner part.

Bar *214*. In FE and GE the $D\sharp^1$ is missing from the chord at the beginning of the bar.

Bar *221*. FE lacks the grace note F^1.

Bars *226—227*. It is very doubtful whether the semiquaver figures, either here or at bars 230—231 and 234—237, are to be understood as sextuplets, as would appear from the sign 6 found in FE (though not in GE) over each of these groups. They are interpreted in this way by, among others, Klindworth, who divides them into two semiquaver triplets. However, we have seen in the note on bar 200 that Chopin used to mark such quaver triplets with a sextuplet sign (which strictly consists of two semiquaver triplets). We see the same at bars 250 and 251, where six semiquavers phrased in pairs are marked with a sextuplet sign. The sextuplets at bar 226 etc., taken on their own, seem to consist of two linked groups, each consisting of three semiquavers, of which the first one is the highest and the following two descend by step. Yet they are derived from figures having augmented values in bars 222—225, where the 3 time signature makes them into three groups of two notes, even in the passages where Chopin introduces a subsidiary 6 time by holding the fourth quaver (bars 224, 225). The addition of the crotchet tails in GE (though they are not found in FE) clearly indicates that the 3 time continues, by phrasing the notes in pairs. For instance the figure at bar 227:

is a faster repetition of the figure at bar 222:

(cf. also bar 228:

and bars 211—213, where, despite the apparent division into threes, the 3 rhythm is certainly preserved).

Bar *242*. For the first quaver in the third triplet FE has the chord $C^2\text{-}E\flat\text{-}C^3$ without the $A\flat^2$.

Bars *243—248*. Unlike FE, GE places the semiquavers in the right hand not over the third quavers of the triplets, but after them. Mikuli does the same.

Bar *244*. The third quaver of the first triplet consists in GE of $E\flat^2\text{-}A\flat^2\text{-}C^3$, and not $F^2\text{-}A\flat^2\text{-}C^3$; in the chord on the fifth quaver, the F^2 is missing.

Bar *251*. The octave *D-D* in the last triplet in the left hand is placed in FE an octave higher; the last chord of this triplet has A^1 instead of $F\sharp^1$.

Bars *252—253*. GE has no $C\sharp^1$ in the left hand in the last chord of bar 252 and the first of bar 253. At bar 253 in FE there is no $A\flat^2$ in the third chord in the right hand. GE does not break the slur between the fifth and sixth quavers of bar 253.

Bars *254—281*. Unlike FE, where the semiquavers are written immediately under or over the third quavers of the corresponding triplets, GE and Mikuli consistently write them after the quavers (with the exception of bars 268—271, where GE too makes them simultaneous). A. Cortot, in his edition of this polonaise, presumes that Chopin here used the traditional classical notation, whereby a dotted quaver and semiquaver are used instead of a triplet consisting of a crotchet and a quaver in order to simplify the notation. GE's notation seems to argue against taking the rhythm in this passage in such a way. This is a very difficult problem. The dotted rhythm, which gives the semiquavers their real value in 3-time, seems to be better suited to the character of this passage, with the obvious exception of bars 268—271, where the displacement of the semiquavers in the right hand would create an uneven and unpleasantly discordant sound.

Bar *254*. FE has the bare octave $E\flat^1\text{-}E\flat^2$ without the C^2 for the second and third quavers of the right hand.

Bar *255*. In GE the minim $E\flat^2$ in the right hand is not tied to the one in the preceding bar. For the third quaver, GE repeats only the third $A\flat^1\text{-}C^2$. In the last chord of the bar, FE has $E\flat^1$ and not F^1. This is probably a misprint, since at the corresponding bars 257 and 259 it has F^1 and not $E\flat^1$.

Bar *262*. Instead of the second semiquaver rest in the bass, GE and Mikuli's edition dot the preceding quaver. The first chord in the right hand in FE has an "arpeggio" sign after the grace note. GE does not tie over the $A\flat^2$ at the end of this bar.

Bar *274*. GE brings in the chord $E\flat\text{-}B\flat\text{-}D\flat$ under the semiquaver G^1 in the right hand instead of delaying it, like FE and us, until the second beat. The same happens at bar 276.

Bar *279*. For the last semiquaver in the right hand, FE has $A\flat$ alone. We have followed GE and Mikuli's edition.

8. *Polonaise in D minor, op. 71 No. 1*

Abbreviations: FtE — the first edition by J. Fontana (A. M. Schlesinger, Berlin, No. 4397).

A considerable part of the manuscript of this polonaise was reproduced with Chopin's Contredanse in the "Kuryer Literacko-Naukowy" (The Literary and Scientific Courier), the supplement to No. 265 of the "Illustrowany Kuryer Codzienny" (The Illustrated Daily Courier), Cracow, September 24th,

1934. It seems from the notes to these reproductions that both works were sent to Tytus Woyciechowski in the middle of 1827 (NB. Fontana also mentions 1827 as the year in which the polonaise was composed). As far as can be judged from the reproduction, the manuscripts of both works are autographs. The reproduction gives the main section of the Polonaise and the first part of the trio. It appears from the above mentioned notes to the reproductions that the remainder of the work was not photographed. The original no longer exists. The manuscript of this polonaise shows considerable differences as compared with the text as we have it in the Fontana edition. We do not discuss these differences here, as they are too numerous, and a reproduction from a not very clear photograph often does not enable us to establish the text with complete certainty.

FtE has the metronome marking ♪ = 84, which is obviously a misprint. The quaver should in fact be a crotchet.

In FtE's text the legato and phrasing slurs are very few and far between. The phrasing in the present edition is mostly our own.

Bar 12. Klindworth rearranges the last chords in order to avoid the parallel octaves between the melody and the upper part in the left hand. But these octaves are only a doubling of the melody.

Bar 14 et seq. The fingering of the sextuplets in the left hand of bars 14−16 and the right hand of bar 19 is reproduced from FtE with the exception of the second $G\sharp^2$ (the seventh semiquaver of bar 19), where we have substituted the second finger for the thumb.

Bar 19. In order to emphasize the two melodies implied in the figuration, the notation should be as follows:

Strictly speaking, there are even three parts, because in addition to the lower part, with the rhythm quaver-semiquaver, the upper part has a dual nature. One part links all the upper semiquavers (B^3-$F\sharp^3$-E^3, $F\sharp^3$-E^3-$F\sharp^2$ etc.), and the other leads from the lower semiquaver to the other two in the triplet (D^3-$F\sharp^3$-E^3, $G\sharp^2$-E^3-$F\sharp^2$ etc.).

Bar 41. Chopin could easily have avoided the parallel octaves in the outer parts in the last chords of the bar (e.g. by means of the chords given by Klindworth in his edition). Still, in his later works, Chopin did not hesitate to use similar parallel progressions; here, moreover, the progression is softened by the retardation of the upper part.

Bar 46. In the last chord we have changed the $E\sharp^1$, found in FtE, to F^1, in view of the chord's subsequent resolution ($G\sharp$-B-D-F to A-$C\sharp$-E with the added seventh G). The same applies to bar 82.

Bar 59. Some recent editions have D, and not $D\sharp$, in the treble throughout the whole bar (unlike bar 57). We reproduced FtE's version.

Bar 60 et seq. Klindworth notates the figuration in bar 60 and the subsequent bars as follows:

Yet more appropriate would be the following:

because it suggests the most natural way of executing the figures, especially in quick tempo.

Bar 61. Recent editions have B^2 for the first semiquaver in the right hand, and not $B\sharp^2$. The same applies to the first note of the last triplet in the bar.

Bar 62. FtE has G and not $F\sharp\sharp$ in the bass. The same applies to the last triplet of bar 66 in the treble. FtE has D^1-$E\sharp^1$ and not $E\sharp^1$-A^1 at the beginning of the bar in the treble. We have followed Mikuli's version.

Bars 62−68. We have reproduced the slurring in the left hand from the Scholtz' edition.

Bar 67. FtE has E^3 and not $D\sharp^3$ as the fourth note from the end of the bar. We have followed Mikuli's version.

Bars 70−71. FtE consistently writes A instead of $G\sharp\sharp$.

Bar 72. FtE has C instead of $B\sharp$ in the second triplet.

9. Polonaise in B♭ major, op. 71 No. 2

Abbreviations: FtE — the first edition by J. Fontana (A. M. Schlesinger, Berlin, No. 4398). The phrasing is our own.

Bar 4. FtE has no G in the last chord.

Bar 5. FtE indicates *piano* instead of *forte*, probably erroneously.

Bar 9. FtE notates the lead into bar 10 in the left hand as follows:

We have followed the version given at bar 37.

Bar 10. At the end of the bar FtE has the following bass:

Bar 38 is similar.

Bars 12−13. In contrast to the similar thirds between bars 13 and 14, FtE does not tie the thirds between bars 12 and 13 (and 40—41). It is very probable that the absence of ties is inadvertent.

Bar 15. FtE ties the *E♭*'s in the first two chords in the bass as at bar 43, and once in the recapitulation, but the second chord in the bar always has an "arpeggio" sign from the *E♭* upwards. We have accepted Mikuli's version.

Bar 17. At the end of the bar FtE has the following notation in the left hand:

Bar 45 is similar.

Bar 18. At the end of the bar FtE has the following notation in the left hand:

Bar 46 is similar.

Bars 26, 28 and 30. We retain the rhythmic variations in the final thirds of these bars, as being very characteristic of Chopin's freedom and variety.

Bars 27 and 29. FtE curtails the second *F* in the bass (and the second *G* at bars 31 and 32). In these bars and at bar 31 we have left the endings of the trills in the right-hand part as they are given in all the recent editions, including Mikuli's. It should be mentioned, however, that FtE does not have these endings, and it is very likely that in these passages Chopin intended only a mordent (as seems to be certain in the case of the notes marked *tr.* in bars 26, 28, and similar bars) — the more so as the execution of the trills in the inner part presents some difficulty.

Bars 34 and 35. FtE has no *C¹* in the chord at the beginning of these and later corresponding bars

Bar 53. FtE here has:

as in the subsequent repetitions of these bars and at bar 54, though in the repetitions of the latter bar FtE does not tie the *D*'s either in the bass or in the treble. At bars 69—70, FtE has a similar notation to that at bar 53, but without the "arpeggio" signs.

Bar 59. FtE has *D♭¹* instead of *C♯¹* at the end of the bar.

Bars 63—64. We have accepted Klindworth's slurring. FtE slurs each triplet, as at bars 65—66.

Bars 73—74. FtE ties the thirds *D¹-F¹* between bars 73 and 74, but does not tie the similar thirds at bars 77—78.

Bar 80. In contrast to bar 79, FtE does not give the ending of the trill. Some recent editions add the notes $A\sharp^3$-$B\sharp^3$. Others, following Mikuli, add only $A\sharp^3$, avoiding the repetition of B^3 at the beginning of bar 81. It is probable, however, that Chopin meant to end the trill on its upper note, $C\sharp^4$, and then go straight on to the B^3 in the following bar.

10. Polonaise in F minor, op. 71 No. 3

Abbreviations: FtE — first edition by J. Fontana (A. M. Schlesinger, Berlin, No. 4399). MS. — Chopin's autograph in the collection of the Frederick Chopin Society in Warsaw. At the end of the autograph there is a remark by Chopin: *Mille pardons pour la mauvaise écriture. FCH Stuttgard 1836.* The writing is, however, clear and legible. The text differs considerably in many details from that given in FtE, as to both the notes and the phrasing, as well as other indications and signs, which are very numerous. The pedalling is given only for bars 15—17 and 27—28, with the sign to lift the pedal under the rests at the ends of these bars. Bars 51—72 and 92—99 are marked in MS. only as repeats of the corresponding preceding bars. We consider below only the more important differences between MS. and FtE. When Chopin wanted to send a copy of this polonaise to Eliza Radziwiłł, he asked Woyciechowski (in his letter of 14th November 1829) to send him one, adding: "I do not want to write it out from memory..., as I should probably write it differently". But it is not likely that Chopin had a copy of the polonaise with him in Stuttgart on his journey in 1836. We may assume that he wrote it out from memory, which would explain the differences between MS. and FtE.

The phrasing is ours. In MS. and FtE it is very fragmentary.

Bar 2. In MS. the second crotchet in the bass, *A♭*, is preceded by its lower octave in the form of a grace note; and, in the corresponding chord in the right hand, the *C* is written as a minim and not repeated at the end of the bar.

Bar 5. In FtE the sign *ten.* is given under the *D♭²*. We believe, however, that this sign is meant to apply to the *F* in the bass, which should be held throughout the whole bar. MS. has neither the sign *ten.*, nor *tr.*; but it gives *espress.*

Bar 8. After the semiquavers *G¹-A♭¹-G¹-A♭¹*, MS. repeats the *G¹* and *A♭¹* as grace notes before the *B♭¹* (cf. bar 38).

Bar 10. In MS., *B♭¹* in the treble is notated as a crotchet followed by a quaver rest.

Bar 11. MS. does not have the grace note either at the beginning or at the end of the bar. Klindworth changed the grace note *A♭¹* (the first note in the right hand) to a *B♭¹*, possibly quite rightly, as Chopin very rarely has grace notes at the same pitch as their principal notes. The last two notes in the right hand (Ab^1-A^1) are notated by Klindworth as ♪♪

B a r *12*. In MS. the first note in the right hand is A^1.

B a r *13*. MS. has *forte*; before the Gb^2 with the *tr.* at the beginning of the bar, it has as grace notes F^1-Gb^1, and after the Gb^1 there is a run from F^1 to F^2 notated in small quavers and marked *con forza*.

B a r *14*. MS. does not have the mordent.

B a r s *15—22*. In MS. the first note in the left hand in these bars is a single C, written as a quaver and followed by a quaver rest.

B a r *16*. MS. lacks the grace note at the end of the bar.

B a r s *19—22*. In the left hand of bars 19 and 20, FtE has Cb^1 instead of B, and similarly for the seventh semiquaver of bar 20 it has Cb^3 instead of B^2. On the third beat of bars 19 and 21, FtE has crotchets in the bass. We have retained the notation that corresponds to the preceding bars. On the third beat of bars 19 and 20 MS. has Cb^1 alone (as a quaver followed by a quaver rest). On the third beat of bars 21 and 22 it has only a crotchet G; however the thirds above the semiquavers are given in bars 19 and 20 as dotted crotchets and in bars 21 and 22 as minims.

B a r s *23* and *24*. The fingering of the bass line is to be found in FtE, as is that of the first chord in the right hand. We have followed FtE's arrangement of the parts. The recent editions give the G in the chord at the beginning of these bars to the left hand. In MS. the turn has a stroke through it, which means that it should begin on the $D\sharp$; recent editions have the same version. FtE does not mark the sharp. Brugnoli has D^1, which is incorrect. However Brugnoli rightly recommends beginning the turn on the principal note E^1 (as does Mikuli). Klindworth and Scholtz begin it on the F^1 above, which is inconsistent, since at bar 18 they begin on the principal note, C^2. A similar version is also given in MS., where the turn is written out in small notes.

B a r s *25* and *26*. In MS. the rhythm of the grace notes in these bars is notated exactly: at bar 25 the F^1 and G^1 are written as quavers and followed by semiquavers, and at bar 26 the G is a dotted quaver and followed by demisemiquavers. Recent editions have demisemiquavers at all three places.

B a r s *28, 29, 31—33*. The fingering is reproduced from FtE (with the exception of the G^2 in bar 28, where FtE indicates the fifth finger, and the first note of bar 32, Ab^2, where FtE has the fourth finger).

B a r s *29—30* and *33—34*. In MS., the last quaver in the left hand of bars 29 and 30 is not a bare octave but a chord F-C^1-Ab^1. Similarly at bars 33 and 34 — Bb-F^1-Db^2.

B a r *37*. The left hand in MS. is quite different from FtE's: it first has D twice (without the natural), then Bb and F-F^1, and finally Eb-Bb and Gb-Eb^1.

B a r *40*. FtE has $D\sharp^2$ and not Eb^2 at the beginning of the bar in the right hand; and it ties this note to the following Eb^2. Mikuli has D^2 instead of $D\sharp^2$. The fingering of the first three semiquavers is reproduced from FtE. In MS. this bar runs as follows:

B a r s *44—50*. In these bars MS. indicates *sempre più piano dim. e poco rallentando*.

B a r s *47—50*. In MS., the ₁C at the beginning of bar 47 in the right hand is tied to the one at the end of bar 46; however it is dotted, as are the C^2 and the C^3 at the beginning of bars 48 and 49. In the right hand of bar 50, after a quaver C^2 (which is dotted but tied to the preceding C^2), MS has a quaver C^1, followed by a crotchet ₁C and then a crotchet rest. In the left hand, however, MS. has two quaver chords, C-F-G, and then a quaver rest, after which, below the thirds G-Bb, F-Ab and E-G, it has a C as a dotted crotchet.

B a r *77*. MS. has no Bb^1 below the quaver Db^2 on the third beat of the bar in the right hand; and in the left hand it has a crotchet E, followed by Bb-Db^1 as the last quaver of the bar. Klindworth changes the bass at the end of the bar, as given at a), and Scholtz as given at b):

Both these versions certainly sound better than FtE's. The last G^1 in the right hand is given by FtE as a semiquaver, and followed by a semiquaver rest. At bar 96 FtE notates this G^1 as a quaver, despite this, however, still adding a semiquaver rest.

B a r s *77—79*. The fingering for the right hand at bar 77 (semiquavers 2—8), at bar 78 and at the beginning of bar 79 is reproduced from FtE.

B a r *78*. MS. does not have the grace note Bb^1. The minim is written as Cb^2 and given an accent and a figure 3, to indicate the fingering, although the preceding Bb^1 has the same fingering. FtE also writes the minim as Cb^2.

B a r s *80—81*. Instead of Fb^1 FtE has E^1. The grace notes should be executed as at bar 25 (see above). In MS. the second note in the treble is given as a semiquaver E^1. On the second beat of the bar MS. has the sixth Db^1-Bb^1, and on the third beat the sixth C^1-Ab^1, notated as a quaver and followed by a quaver rest. In the left hand MS. has no Bb at the beginning of the bar. On the second beat of the bar it has a quaver rest and $E\flat$ alone, and on the third beat the octave $A\flat$-$A\flat$ and a quaver rest. MS. does not have bar 81, i.e. it has no "second time" version for the repeat.

B a r *82.* At the beginning of the bar MS. has only $E\flat^{3}$, written as a quaver and tied to the first note of the sextuplet. In FtE, the second note in the sextuplet is notated as B^{1}.

B a r *83.* MS. has the grace notes F^{2}-$E\flat^{2}$ as demi-semiquavers following a dotted quaver; MS. does not have either the turn or the grace note $D\flat^{2}$. In MS. the crotchet $D\flat^{3}$ at the end of the bar is tied to the $D\flat^{3}$ at the beginning of bar 84 where, however, the grace note is not given.

B a r *84.* FtE and MS. give the fourth semiquaver an additional quaver tail. In MS. the first three and the last notes of the sextuplet have additional upper tails which are joined with a ligature.

B a r *86.* In MS. the right-hand part runs as follows:

B a r *88.* In MS. the right-hand part runs as follows:

In FtE the penultimate semiquaver is given as $C\flat^{3}$.

B a r *89.* The last four semiquavers in the bar in MS. consist of the thirds C^{3}-$E\flat^{3}$ and D^{3}-F^{3}, each repeated. The second quaver in the left hand in MS. is C^{1}-$E\flat^{1}$-G^{1} (obviously a misprint for $D\flat^{1}$-$E\flat^{1}$-G^{1}), the third is $A\flat$-$A\flat^{1}$, and the last A-$E\flat^{1}$-$G\flat^{1}$.

B a r *91.* In MS. the second note on the second beat of the bar, $E\flat^{2}$, is written as a demisemiquaver, following a dotted semiquaver. The second beat of the bar in the left hand has only $E\flat^{1}$.

11. Polonaise in G minor

Published in 1817, reprinted from the only known copy in Z. Jachimecki's book *F. Chopin et son oeuvre*, Paris 1930, pp. 45—47; next edited by Jachimecki in the collection *Trzy polonezy z lat naj-młodszych* (Three Polonaises from the Earliest Years), Cracow 1947. Our edition is based on the text as it is known from these two publications. The reprint in Jachimecki's book is denoted by R, and his edition by JE. We ourselves have added phrasing, dynamics etc., partly reproduced from JE.

B a r *8.* R and JE have a natural before the grace note E^{3}. This sign was probably misprinted (or misread) instead of a flat, which would restore the $E\flat$ after the E at the end of the preceding bar.

B a r s *11—12.* JE gives the left-hand part at the end of bar 11 and the beginning of bar 12 as follows:

The typographical error (crotchets instead of quavers) at the beginning of bar 12 aside, we feel that R authorizes us to accept the more appropriate $E\flat^{1}$ instead of $F\sharp^{1}$ in the last chord of bar 11, and D^{1} instead of $F\sharp^{1}$ in the second chord of bar 12 (cf. the second chord of bars 22, 30 and 38). The last two notes in the melody at bars 12, 22, 30 and 38 are written in R in such a way that the last note is a minim and the preceding one a crotchet grace note.

B a r *13.* The top note in the second chord in JE is C^{2} and not A^{1}. We prefer A^{1}, which is to be found in R and corresponds to the $F\sharp^{1}$ at bar 1, because bars 13—16 are an exact transposition of bars 1—4 into B♭ major.

B a r *22.* R does not indicate *Fine* either here or at bar 12. Nor does it have the repeat of the main section of the polonaise after bar 22. It is virtually impossible, however, that Chopin really wished to end the polonaise at bar 22 in a foreign key. In our opinion, the first section should be repeated after the second, but omitting the introduction (bars 1—4). This corresponds to the usual form adopted in Chopin's early polonaises, in the Polonaises in G♯ minor and G♭ major, in all three polonaises of op. 71, etc. The omission of the introduction is the more advisable here since the second section contains the introduction transposed. After the trio, however, the polonaise should obviously be repeated from the beginning.

B a r *29.* The turn should be played like this:

12. *Polonaise in B♭ major (composed in 1817)*

Edited by Jachimecki from the manuscript and published in the "Kuryer Literacko-Naukowy" (Literary and Scientific Courier) in Cracow, a supplement to the "Illustrowany Kuryer Codzienny" (The Illustrated Daily Courier), January 22nd, 1934, together with the facsimile which we denote by F and subsequently in the collection *Trzy Polonezy z lat najmłodszych* (Three Polonaises from the Earliest Years), Cracow 1947. This latter edition is denoted by JE.

With the exception of the *forte* at the beginning of the work, and short slurs in the treble at bars 23, 24, 29 and 30, F has no phrasing, dynamics, etc.

B a r *12.* As in the Polonaise in G minor, F gives the last note of the melody as a minim and the preceding note as a crotchet grace note. Similarly at bars 20 and 32.

B a r *13*. Here and at bar 17 the turn should be executed as follows:

and at bar 15 like this:

B a r *20*. As in the Polonaise in G minor, it is doubtful whether this polonaise should end with the second section, without a repeat of the main section. F gives no indications as to this. The repeat of the main section (with the omission of the introduction, i. e. bars 1—4) is less obviously indicated here than in the Polonaise in G minor because the second section ends in the home key.

B a r s *32* and *42*. F and JE give the penultimate chord an additional A^1 between the $F\sharp^1$ and the C^2. We have made the cadence conform to that of bars 12 and 20.

B a r *36*. We recommend altering the bass as follows:

F indicates *Dal segno*. JE has the appropriate sign at the beginning of the trio at bar 21; but in F this sign is to be found at the beginning of bar 27, i. e. only the second half of the main section of the trio is to be repeated, as in the trio in the Polonaise in G minor.

13. Polonaise in Ab major (dedicated to Żywny)

Composed in 1821, published by Gebethner and Wolff, Warsaw, in 1902, according to J. Michałowski's transcription. The original version was published in the music supplement to the first number of "Die Musik" in Berlin in 1908 and in Brugnoli's edition (Ricordi, Milan). It has recently been published by Z. Jachimecki in the collection *Trzy Polonezy z lat najmłodszych* (Three Polonaises from the Earliest Years), Cracow, 1947. Our edition is based mainly on the reproduction of the manuscript (denoted by MS.) in Hoesick's book *Chopin. Życie i Twórczość* (Chopin, His Life and Art), 1910, vol. I, p. 43.

MS. contains no instructions, phrasing or accents except *ritard.* at bars 25 and 50.

B a r *1*. Brugnoli recommends beginning the turn on the lower note, i.e. on D^3. We think, however, that he is wrong and that the turn should begin on F^3. In Brugnoli's and Jachimecki's editions the last note of the melody in bar 1 is a third higher than in our edition, i.e. Ab^3. We have accepted F^3, following the version in "Die Musik"; MS. seems rather to favour this.

B a r *4*. Instead of the third G^1-Bb^1 in the **right** hand Brugnoli has only G^1, and Jachimecki only Bb^1.

B a r *6*. MS. has Db^2 instead of $C\sharp^2$.

B a r *12*. Neither MS. nor the other editions give the ending of the trill, either here or at bar 46 at the cadence of the trio.

B a r *16*. Brugnoli and Jachimecki do not have the Ab^2 on the third quaver in the treble. MS. and "Die Musik", however, do have this note, which corresponds to the Gb in bar 20.

B a r s *21—23*. MS. has an erroneous E^1 instead of Fb^1 in the chords of the left hand.

B a r *40*. MS. has Gb^2 instead of $F\sharp^2$.

14. Polonaise in G♯ minor

Published for the first time in 1864 by B. Schotts Söhne in Mainz. Included in the collected editions of Gebethner and Wolff in Warsaw (vol. III, No. 13) and Breitkopf & Härtel in Leipzig (vol. XIII, No. 15). It is also to be found in the editions by Mikuli, Kullak, Pugno, Brugnoli and others. It bears the inscription *Dédiée à Madame Dupont*, probably a member of a family known to Chopin in Warsaw (Chopin mentions Mademoiselle Dupont in his letter to T. Woyciechowski, dated May 15th, 1830). Niecks, in his book *F. Chopin as a Man and Musician* (II, 1902, p. 243), very sensibly questions the date of composition of this polonaise (1822). The style and developed technique of the piece seem to indicate a much later period in Chopin's work. We have replaced the very imprecise phrasing in Breitkopf & Härtel's edition by phrasing taken mostly from Kullak's and Brugnoli's editions. We have kept the signs and dynamic indications of the earliest editions, although the majority of them were probably added by the editors.

B a r *3*. In Mikuli's and Brugnoli's editions the $G\sharp$'s on the third and fourth quavers in the right hand are not tied. We have retained the version in Breitkopf & Härtel's edition, though we think that it is still better to tie the B as well, thus:

as in Pugno's edition.

B a r *6*. Mikuli, Kullak, Pugno and Brugnoli recommend that the trill should begin on the principal note. But a different opinion is tenable in view of the fact that the note before the trill is also E^3, so that it is possible to begin on the upper note, $F\sharp^3$. The same applies to the trill at bar 35.

B a r *30*. Breitkopf & Härtel's edition does not have the double sharp before the twelfth demisemiquaver.

15. Polonaise in Bb minor

Composed before leaving for Reinertz (Duszniki) in 1826. Published in the "Echo Muzyczne" (Musical

Echo) of June 3rd, 1881, No. 12, music supplement, pp. 89—95, and then included in the collected edition of Gebethner and Wolff (vol. III, No. 15) in Warsaw, and in the collected edition of Breitkopf & Härtel in Leipzig (vol. XIII, No. 16). It is also to be found in the editions of Kullak (published by Schlesinger in Berlin), Brugnoli (Edizione Ricordi in Milan) and others. Beyond the indication *Con Ped.* at the beginning of the trio, the first edition has no pedalling. This has been added by us.

B a r *8*. In contrast to bar 38, the turn is notated in the first editions ("Echo Muzyczne", Gebethner and Breitkopf) not as a sextuplet of demisemiquavers, but as a number of grace notes grouped around the quaver F^1:

Brugnoli here claims to see an intentional rhythmic differentiation in these two different notations. In our opinion, the meaning and the execution of these embellishments is exactly the same in both cases, and for this reason we give a uniform notation.

B a r s *11—12*. In the first editions of this polonaise the first semiquaver in each bar is separated from the following notes, being given its own tail.

B a r *14*. The first editions do not divide this passage between the hands.

B a r *18*. In the first editions, the turn is given with A^2 as the principal note and G^2 as the lower note. Kullak has it as follows:

It would be most natural, however, for the turn to have A^2 as the principal note and $G\sharp^2$ as the lower note, or $A\flat^2$ as the principal note and G^2 as the lower.

B a r *25*. The first editions have no F in the second chord in the left hand.

B a r *43*. In contrast to bar 59, the demisemiquaver F^2 appears in the first editions as a single note, without the chord.

B a r *45*. Here and at bar 61, following Kullak's edition, we tie the $A\flat^2$'s in the last two chords in the right hand by analogy with bars 8 and 33.

B a r *49*. At the beginning of the bar, Gebethner and Wolff's edition has $D\flat^1$ and not $B\flat$ as the top note of the chord in the left hand. We have preferred by analogy the version of bar 47.

B a r *51*. The first editions have $D\flat^2$-C^2-$C\flat^2$-$B\flat^1$ as the first semiquavers in the left hand.

16. Polonaise in G♭ major

This polonaise was published for the first time by B. Schotts Söhne in Mainz in 1872, and then appeared in the collected edition of Gebethner and Wolff in 1883 (vol. III, No. 14) and in the supplement to the first number of "Die Musik" in Berlin, in 1908/9. It was also reprinted in R. Pugno's edition of the Polonaises (Universal-Edition).

The authenticity of this polonaise has been questioned by F. Niecks (*F. Chopin as a Man and Musician*, II, 1902, p. 359), and has been discussed by Jachimecki in the Proceedings of the Polish Academy of Science (vol. XXXIX, 1934, No. 1).

We have based our edition on the text published in "Die Musik". We have supplemented and modified the phrasing in some passages, and have added the pedalling.

B a r *I*. Pugno gives the tempo as *Allegro moderato* ♩ = 84.

B a r s *9* and *11*. The endings of the trills have been added by us.

B a r *13*. "Die Musik" has no $E\flat\flat$ at bar 13, but only $E\flat$. In view of the exactness of the repetition in all other details in this section it is very improbable that there should be an intentional variant here.

B a r *20*. The end of the bar in the right hand is notated in "Die Musik" as follows:

We adopt the notation given at bar 50.

B a r *28*. In the "Die Musik" edition the first note in the left hand, $D\flat$, is a minim, as at bar 58. In the repeat of the first section of the polonaise the upbeat $D\flat^1$ should probably be played at the end of bar 28, as at bar 8. "Die Musik", however, does not indicate this.

B a r *35*. Our original has the indication *al termoda*. This undoubtedly ought to be *tre corde* (after *una corda* at bar 33), as given in Pugno's edition.

B a r s *59* and *60*. The *tr.* signs in these bars should be interpreted as mordents. The similar signs at bar 61, however, mean longer trills, with endings.

B a r *71*. "Die Musik" has the same rhythm in the accompaniment as in the following bar. In the repeat of this section at bar 122 however the rhythm is: ♪ ♫♫ ♪ .

B a r s *101*, *103*, *105* and *107*. The endings of the trills have been added by us.

D R L U D W I K   B R O N A R S K I
Fribourg (Switzerland)
P R O F. J Ó Z E F T U R C Z Y Ń S K I
Morges